The Weeping Woman

The Weeping Woman
Encounters with La Llorona

Compiled and Edited by
Edward Garcia Kraul and
Judith Beatty

Illustrations by Tony Sanchez

The Word Process
Santa Fe, New Mexico 87502

First Edition/Printed in the United States of America
1 2 3 4 5 6 7 8 9 10 — 94 93 92 91 90 89 88

ISBN 0-945937-06-7 Softcover
Library of Congress Catalog Card Number: 88-50347

Book design by Suzette Mahr, Words & Deeds,
Los Angeles, CA 90065
Cover design by Chris Lopez and Larry Brito,
Artline Graphics, Las Vegas, NM 87701
Technical Assistance from ComputerLand,
Santa Fe, NM 87501
Printed by BookCrafters, Chelsea, MI 48118

Published by
The Word Process
P.O. Box 5699
Santa Fe, New Mexico 87502-5699
(505) 988-3465

Acknowledgments

There are so many people who have shown continued interest in our project from its very inception that it would be impossible to name them all. There are also many kind-hearted people living in the villages of northern New Mexico who directed us to someone's home, or who gave us a cup of coffee, or who simply told us how much they liked the idea that someone was putting together a book narrated by the natives who live with *La Llorona* stories in their midst. It is regrettable that we do not know their names for the most part, but we send a "thank you" to them, wherever they are. We do want to thank some "special" folks, however: Manuel Alcon; Carlos Araujo; Jerome Beatty, Jr.; Greg Cook; Blanche and Joe D'Igalo; Jimmy and Nora Gallegos; Victoria Krueger; Denise and Mike Lamb; Bobette Perrone; Alice Sena; and Eloy and Rose Zamora.

Additionally, we wish to extend our warmest thanks to all of the people who donated the stories in these pages, as well as to those whose stories we could not use for one reason or another.

And, finally, special thanks beyond measure to Ramon M. Candelaria at Sunwest Bank, Santa Fe; and Juan Valdez, Assistant to the Santa Fe City Manager, Santa Fe, New Mexico.

Este libro ha sido preparado con el proposito de que sirva de ayuda a las generaciones futuras de origen hispano residentes en los Estados Unidos. Es lamentable que la poblacion hispana en estos tiempos se ha estado olvidando de sus tradiciones pasadas. Este libro es dedicado a esta generacion presente, lo mismo que a las futuras con la esperanza de que les sirva para que no se olviden de estas tradiciones: de las cuales, "Las Leyendas de La Llorona" tienen un papel bastante importante.

Expresamos nuestra gratitud a toda la gente que ha contribuido y ayudado para que la publicacion de este libro haya sido posible.

And was there until the death
of Herod: that it might be fulfilled
which was spoken of the Lord by
the prophet, saying, Out of Egypt
have I called my son.

Then Herod, when he saw that
he was mocked of the wise men,
was exceeding wroth, and sent forth,
and slew all the children that were
in Bethlehem, and in all the coasts
thereof, from two years old and
under, according to the time which
he had diligently inquired of the
wise men.

Then was fulfilled that which
was spoken by Jeremy the prophet,
saying,

In Rama was there a voice
heard, lamentation, and weeping, and
great mourning, Rachel weeping for
her children, and would not be
comforted, because they are not.

Matthew 2:15-18

Contents

Foreword   xi

The Owl at the Cemetery
   Yvonne C. Roybal   1

Los Dientes
   Julian Grace   3

The Lady Gambler
   Victor Cortez   5

She Laments But No One Listens
   Manuel B. Alcon   7

The Illustrator's Nightmare
   Tony Sanchez   10

Lassoing La Llorona
   T. J. Chavez   13

La Llorona Escapes from the Police
   Cosme Garcia   14

The Hitchhiker
   Ray Lucero   15

Los Tecolotes en el Techo
   Margarita Olivas   17

Frozen on the River
   Robert V. Montoya   18

The Haunting of Pojoaque
   Stephen W. Long   19

La Llorona Almost Hangs
   Frank Maloof   21

The 'R' Car to Tortilla Flats
   Edward Garcia Kraul   24

The Horse That Left No Tracks
   Carlos Valdez   26

The Test Drive
   Waylon Tuttle   28

The Haunting of Placita Rafaela
    Phil Griego   31

Ralph Martinez' Long Ride Home
    Juan Dominguez   32

El Molino
    Alfonso "Trompo" Trujillo   34

The Llorona
    Melisendro Apodaca   35

The Sheepherder Takes a Bath
    Irene Ortiz   36

Aunt Aga as La Llorona
    Margie Ulibarri   39

La Llorona Gets Shot
    Victor Cortez   41

Mourning at Rosario Cemetery
    Irene Ortiz   43

Ramon Garcia's Last Date
    Fred "El Gallina" Montoya   45

The Road from Puerta de Luna
    Ernest Lucero   46

El Borracho on the Santa Fe River
    El Enano   48

El Rancho de Los Maranos
    Isidro Guerrero   51

Great Balls of Fire
    Demetrio Lujan   55

The Courtyard Fantasy
    George O. Tate   57

Terrorizing Las Colonias
    Joann Baca   60

El Dia de San Geronimo y La Noche de La Llorona
    Fred "El Gallina" Montoya   63

Eduardo
    Sam Welch   65

Contents *(continued)*

The Man Who Wouldn't Go to Church
  Ruben Chavez   67
The Ride from El Ojo de La Vaca
  Juanita Garcia   71
The Hippie Learns a Lesson
  Refugio Archuleta   73
The Mystery of Ramona Sena
  John R. Sandoval   76
The Woman in White
  Patricio Lujan   79
The Best Horseman of All
  Cosme Garcia   82
Sister Cleo's Revelation
  Orlinda Tapia   85
The Rabbit Coat
  Maclovia Guerin   87
La Llorona de La Junta
  Barbara Berger   90
The Robe
  Robert Gonzales   92
Uncle Manuel and La Llorona
  Juanita Garcia   96
The Last Dance
  Herman Grace   98
The Tiny Screamer
  Alfonso "Trompo" Trujillo   101
Ruben and Max
  Raymond Lovato   104
Postscript
  Lisa Sena   106

Foreword

La Llorona, "the weeping woman," is as well known to the descendants of the Spaniards in the Hispanic world as the bogey-man is to some Anglo cultures. And, there are probably as many different stories of this legendary phantom woman as there are people who tell them. As customs and traditions vary from village to village or from one region to the next, so do the versions of *La Llorona* and her plight as she searches in vain for her lost children. While *La Llorona* can be found in Celtic and North African cultures (as well as in the Bible), certainly the most haunting, memorable, and terrifying tales of all seem to come from the American Southwest.

Before Hernando Cortes arrived with his *conquistadores*, the Aztec Indians nightly heard the ghostly screams of Cihuacóatl, a pre-Columbian earth goddess ruling childbirth and death, whose cries of, "My children, we must flee," echoed throughout the stone canyons of Tenochtitlan. Ten years later, her dire warnings came to fruition with the arrival of Cortes. Aiding him in his conquest of the New World was *La Malinche*—"The Tongue"—his beautiful Indian interpreter and mistress whose role of translator facilitated the downfall of her own people. Years later, when Cortes announced to his mistress that he would return to Spain without her but with their young son, *La Malinche* pierced her heart and that of the child's with an obsidian knife. Today, it is believed by many that *La Llorona* and *La Malinche* were one and the same person.

When the northern outpost of the Spanish Empire in America was colonized, the Spanish settlers brought *La Llorona* with them. The tales shared around the campfires during the long trek north from Mexico City can still be heard today from the *visabuelos*—great grandparents—still living in the remote villages of the Southwest, and the stories continue through the generations in rich variety.

Of all of the variations heard today, the most popular one conjures up an image of the modern *La Llorona* in a black or white cloak, sometimes on horseback and sometimes on foot, wandering the arroyos, *acequias* and riverbeds, weeping and wailing for her lost children. Whether these children have been lost, accidentally drowned, or murdered outright by their infamous mother depends upon the storyteller.

Whether *La Llorona* is nine feet tall and floating across a creek, a ball of fire rolling in someone's direction, or a gnomish little person with warts on her nose, she almost always manages to terrorize her wayward victims into some sort of religious conversion or, failing that, into simply changing their ways.

For those who might ask which of the stories that follows is the "real" one, the answer *La Llorona* might offer is this: Whatever your reality is, that is what I am; it is for you, the reader, to decide. As is said in her own tongue, *"Cada cabeza es un mundo*—Each head is its own world."

Denise Mann Lamb
Judith Beatty

The Owl at the Cemetery

In the early 1930's, when the penitentiary was located on Pen Road, and the warden was a man named Swope, a lot of the local people had jobs there and they used to bring home some pretty interesting stories, as you can imagine. It seems hard to believe that this part of town that housed the penitentiary was actually well outside of the city limits.

My grandmother told us that one night, as one of the guards, a guy named Tafoya, was heading home in his car, an owl flew into the headlights and stayed in front of his car as he drove. He became mesmerized by this owl, and started following it. He was powerless to do anything else and the car even seemed to drive itself. It led him to the graveyard over there off of Cordova and Early Street—the Guadalupe Cemetery. He stopped his car when he got there, and just left the lights on, staring through the windshield and watching the owl. The owl was flying all over, in and out among the headstones. It disappeared behind one of them and then all of a sudden, from behind this same headstone appeared a woman dressed all in black, crying and wailing. She came towards him, walking into the headlights while pointing back in the direction of the headstone and indicating that she wanted him to do something, but he couldn't figure out what it was.

He was so terrified that he just sat there, frozen, for what seemed to be an eternity. He eventually got his wits about him, put the car into reverse, backed up as fast as he could, and sped home.

He went back to the cemetery the following day to see what headstone the woman had been pointing at, and he found that it was for an infant that had died at a very tender age—just a few months old.

My grandmother told me it had been *La Llorona* in the cemetery that night, and that she was telling me this story because she didn't want me going into that cemetery or any other cemetery, for that matter. She needn't have worried!

There's more to the story, though. *La Llorona* had quite a reputation in those days—people were always claiming to have seen her, especially after a few drinks at the local *cantina*—and this fellow Tafoya got very excited that he had actually met her face to face, that this was the real thing! The trouble is that no one believed him, not even his own wife or mother. And no matter how he tried to convince them, they just never quite bought the story, even when he took them to the cemetery and pointed out the grave of her child.

It was said that this Tafoya used to wander the streets of the different *barrios* telling the story over and over. And, of course, the more he told it, the less people believed. He left his job and began to spend more and more time at the Guadalupe Cemetery, apparently hoping to see *La Llorona* just once more.

He died at a young age, bewitched by the memory of *La Llorona.*

Yvonne C. Roybal
Los Angeles, CA

 *Los Dientes*

On a warm spring evening in 1945—this was after the war was over—my father, Augustine Grace, and his brother Paul were walking down Romero Street near the railroad tracks where it meets Manhattan. It was about 11:00 p.m. and they were returning home from the pool hall at the Recreation Club. The Recreation Club was on the Plaza and there was a motel upstairs for the tourists.

They had just passed the last house and were almost ready to cross the tracks when my father saw something bright out of the corner of his eye. He turned and saw a ball of fire rolling in their direction. He shouted with surprise and the moment my uncle looked to see what was happening, the ball of fire turned into a bundle wrapped in a patchwork quilt. It stopped dead about 20 feet from them and then just sat there. Suddenly, they heard the sound of a child crying from the bundle. They ran over to it and opened it up and there was this baby about six months old with a terrible, gruesome face and big fangs. It opened its mouth as if to cry, but instead it smiled at them and said, "*Mira, Daddy, tengo dientes*—Look, Daddy, I have teeth." They ran toward West Manhattan, where my dad lived.

When I heard the story, I accused my dad of being drunk. But he wasn't. In fact, he was a man who never lied to anyone. My Uncle Paul developed a white patch on his hair after the experience. Later, all of his hair turned snow white. To this day, they swear it was the child of *La Llorona*.

For many years after that, I had recurring dreams about it. In fact, they were nightmares—I'd wake up in a cold sweat.

In those days, there was a place called the Home Bakery on the corner of Romero and Agua Fria. Whenever there was some extra change, my dad would talk about getting some creme puffs or doughnuts, and I knew they would send me to pick them up. I would have to pass by that spot where *La Llorona's* baby had been seen in order to get to the bakery. There were eight of us, and I was the eldest of the boys and I was supposed to be the bravest. The fact is, I would come up with any excuse I could think of to avoid having to go there. And when I couldn't get out of it, I'd run as fast as I could to get by the spot. Nothing ever happened to me, but it was many years before the bad dreams finally stopped.

Julian Grace
Santa Fe, NM

 # The Lady Gambler

This story was told to me by Emilio Vigil, a gambler from Las Vegas, Nevada:

"Before the big casinos were built and developed for the gamblers in Las Vegas, the old-timers used to gamble in old shacks. The laborers that used to work in this area would spend their time playing blackjack, poker—things like that. At the time this happened it was in the 1940's. This man, a Mr. Gutierrez, and four or five other men were playing cards in one of these old shacks, and some lady came in, very young, very pretty, and she sat down and started gambling with them. It wasn't often that these men ever got to see a young beautiful woman, and this one wasn't like the so-called ladies of the street. She seemed quiet and refined and just expressed a simple and humble interest in joining them at cards. She said something to the effect that gambling was a weakness of hers and she didn't indulge very often.

"She was good, let me tell you. She played the cards like a real professional, and she was flirting with the men at the same time. Well, she cleaned a lot of them out! She sort of left them naked, if you know what I mean. Some men would come in, sit down, and 20 minutes later they would lose their money to her and have to leave.

"After a while, this lady started to tap her foot on Mr. Gutierrez' shoe. She did it just a little, so he wasn't sure if she was doing it on purpose to flirt with him or if it was an accident because she was sitting so close to him at this small table. Being a vain man, however, Mr. Gutierrez figured that she was probably interested in seeing him after the game and was trying to get his attention. So he lifted up the tablecloth to look down at her foot, which was hidden by her long black skirt. At first, he thought that he was seeing things, but then he realized that it was not a shoe,

but a hoof. Like a deer's. It took him a minute to realize that this had to be the *La Llorona* that everyone had been talking about. She had been seen all around the shacks and some of the stories about her said she had a cloven hoof."

Anyway, Mr. Gutierrez told me that he finished playing his hand in the game very quickly. He had already won a lot of money, but he didn't want to stay another minute!

Victor Cortez
Santa Fe, NM

She Laments But No One Listens

Children dear, come sit by my side,
So about La Llorona you may hear.
Also, how she lost her pride
And went all over seeking her lost child
Without a lover.
This story is mild, for La Llorona's life
Was much more wild.
For a woman her size, she put many to trial.

Many centuries ago in Old Spain, a young mother lost her only child. How she came to bring forth her child and how she lost that child is a matter of speculation, for there are as many versions as there are storytellers. As time passes, variations are added to the stories.

The story I'm about to divulge is about the *Llorona* who appeared in the Mora Valley of New Mexico.

If you are acquainted with the Santa Gertrudes Valley, also known as Mora, you know that the Mora River runs through the village and that this river has come to be known as *La Llorona's* highway. But this doesn't mean that she travels or knows any other routes.

Mora is a peaceful valley—most of the time. Sometimes, as you sit on your porch some quiet evening, you will hear a moaning sound. The unbelievers will swear it is the wind brushing against the trees or whatever gets in its way, but that is because they have never seen or met *La Llorona*. To the believers, it is a reality, for they have seen her and they will swear that what they hear is *La Llorona* making her way through the willows or wading in the river, for there are ripples formed there without any other logical explanation.

Many Mora residents will attest to stories about *La Llorona*. This is her home, for she always returns after a brief absence.

There are many cases where people have lost their farm animals or pets, and they will swear that *La Llorona* took them. An instance that comes to mind is the case of a poor farmer in Cleveland, one of the next villages, who lost some sheep and goats. It was reported that *La Llorona* was seen dressed in a sheepskin and crying out loud as she entered the barn where the animals had been locked up for the night. The people who saw this did nothing because they knew it was *La Llorona* and no one was willing to mess around with her. Then, she suddenly disappeared. The following day, two sheep and a goat were missing and there were no signs left behind, such as tracks, so they could investigate.

About this time, little if anything about "child abuse" was known. It was called "discipline" back then, and even if punishment was cruel—which it was, most of the time—parents believed that it was more honorable to cry for a dead child than let that child disgrace the family. Perhaps it is difficult for people to understand now, but the honor of a given family was vitally important and it was expected that each member would uphold the family name through acceptable behavior. Among the methods of controlling unacceptable behavior were woodshed spankings, slaps, and any other means that the older generation could think of. Quite frankly, the one which was the least cruel was calling on *La Llorona* to straighten out the wrongdoer, only because the wrongdoer seldom had to face her and only had to straighten out to avoid the possibility of confrontation.

Lately, very little is said about *La Llorona*, because most people want her dead. But the fact is, she is still very much alive and very real. She hasn't given up her search for her child, but I believe that now she laments the changes and contradictions that present-day life has brought about. For example, people used to go to bed early and get up early. Now, even the owls are put to shame, for people are up at all hours of the day and night. People eat food while they are driving their cars instead of at the dinner table. And where one used to visit friends and neighbors from the neighboring villages, now there is no time to visit; everyone is in a hurry but with no place to go. When one needed to mind Mother Nature's call, one ran outside to the outhouse. Now, one runs into the house. And, where water was once carried into the house for the people, now it is carried outside for the animals. With all of these changes, it is no wonder that *La Llorona* laments alone!

Probably the worst change of all is that now parents are afraid of their own children, and the children are afraid of no one. *La Llorona* does not scare them anymore. The parents no longer go visiting; they are without the family car because their kids are cruising and raising hell. Parents stay home watching television and waiting for their children to get home. *Que vida!* Yes, *La Llorona* still moans and howls, and one can hear her, but alas— no one pays attention to her.

Manuel B. Alcon
Mora, NM

The Illustrator's Nightmare

I was born in Santa Fe and I had polio when I was four so I spend my time in a wheelchair. I have been an artist for 15 years and I work with charcoal, watercolors, oils, you name it. I use my dreams to visualize what I am going to draw. They are an important part of my life.

One day, right after Judith and Eduardo asked me to illustrate this book, I was working on a sketch of a man in a wheelchair being pushed by *La Llorona*. A couple of nights later, after I had gone to bed, this particular illustration became a nightmare for me. I was on my way to the store in my wheelchair, pushing myself along, when suddenly I realized that my wheelchair was moving by itself. I turned my head and saw a tall woman—about six or seven feet. She looked down at me and said, "Tony, you keep telling everybody that you are doing illustrations of me and that you are not a believer— that I'm not real." The terrible thing was that, as she said these words, her mouth didn't move. Then she said, "I will keep appearing in your dreams until you either stop drawing me or start believing." I woke up scared and drained and didn't sleep for the rest of the night.

This nightmare has not stopped me from continuing my drawings of *La Llorona*. I know I will dream of her for a long time because I always dream of all that I see, think, hear, say, or do.

Tony Sanchez
Santa Fe, NM

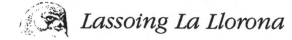 *Lassoing La Llorona*

I used to be Deputy Chief of the New Mexico State Police. I retired in 1985.

When I was growing up, my father, Celso Chavez, who is now deceased, used to tell us stories about things he had witnessed in his younger days. One of the most interesting stories that he told us was that, one lonely night many years ago, as he was riding his horse from El Coyote to Guadalupita, he observed a *bulto*—a form—near the local cemetery that looked like someone dressed in dark clothing, but he could not see the face as it was covered with what looked like a *tapalo*—a shawl. At that point, my father decided to try and lasso this *bulto*, as he had heard so much about *La Llorona*, and he figured, "This must be her." But he couldn't get his horse to run fast enough; he said it was scared and kept rearing back and seemed reluctant to pursue it. So the *bulto* disappeared out of sight.

My father had a lot of guts, and was never afraid of anything, so I can see that he wanted to satisfy himself as to what this *bulto* was.

T. J. Chavez
Santa Fe, NM

La Llorona Escapes
from the Police

I was listening to my shortwave radio one night four years ago, about 1984, and I had the police frequency on. I don't know what time it was, but it was late, when I heard this report that a lady in the El Torreon addition had called the police because she said she could hear *La Llorona* crying from down by the Santa Fe River.

There was a big rush to get over there—you wouldn't believe it! Five police cars and three sheriff's cars. Well, I sat there for about a half hour listening to the transmissions—it was really something. They'd hear crying by a tree, and they'd go over there, and there wouldn't be anything. Then they'd hear it from somewhere else, and they'd all run over there, and of course there wouldn't be anything there, either. They were saying it sounded like a baby crying. You would have thought with all the transmitting back and forth that this was *Fiestas* or some other big event.

Finally, after about a half an hour, one of them said over the radio, "We're never going to find her because it's *La Llorona*." And that was the end of it. They all left.

Believe me, it happened—someone should go see if it's still in their records. I'll bet they erased it.

> Cosme Garcia
> Santa Fe, NM

 *The Hitchhiker*

During the winter of 1953, I stopped at Joe's Ringside in Las Vegas, New Mexico to watch the strip show and have a few beers. It was cold, and I was tired of driving. I was on my way home to La Joya from Denver. My dad, Antonio Lucero, had a small place in La Joya about two or three miles from the Pecos River near the Greer Garson ranch. I had decided to spend the Christmas holidays there with Dad and my two brothers.

Around 11:00 or 11:30 p.m., I left Joe's Ringside and continued to La Joya. As I was driving down the hill towards Tecolote, the bright lights from my Ford illuminated the figure of a woman on the side of the road. In those days, the road was a single lane, one way, and not the big freeway that is there now. I thought to myself, "What is this nun doing on the highway in the middle of the night?" Her dress was a habit of the Catholic nuns I was familiar with. I pulled the car over to a stop and reached over to open the door on the passenger's side. I asked her if she wanted a ride, and she got in the car without saying a word. I could see now that it wasn't a habit she was wearing but a dark cloak with a hood that covered most of her face. I really couldn't even see if she was young or old, or what. We passed through Bernal, San Juan, San Jose, all without her opening her mouth. I didn't mind; I was tired and didn't much feel like talking myself. Still, I tried to be polite a couple of times and ask her some questions, but she never answered me. She sat completely still, much like a mannequin in a store window, with one hand on her knee and the other hidden under her cloak.

When we got to the Pecos cutoff, I was starting to get uncomfortable. Frankly, there was something about her I didn't feel right about. I began to imagine that maybe she had a knife, or maybe she wasn't even a woman but a boy who was going to rob me. I had a big wad of bills in my pocket. I thought to myself, "What if she saw the money at the bar? Maybe he or she was in there."

As if that wasn't enough, I began to imagine the smell of sulphur, like after you've lit a match, but much stronger. That was enough for me. I stopped the car in front of Adelo's store and turned to tell him or her to get out of the car, but she had disappeared in thin air. Without opening the door. Then I heard this blood-curdling yell, very high-pitched—terrible. It raised the hair on my neck; that's the truth. Even the dogs ran off.

I told this story to some guys at the Sunshine Bar and a guy— I don't remember his name, Freddie something—said the exact same thing had happened to some other sucker a couple of weeks before. Then he said to me, "That was *La Llorona, mula!*"

Ray Lucero
Pecos, NM

Los Tecolotes en el Techo

I was born in 1909 here in Mora. I live by the church in the area they now call China, by some *acequias*. I lived in Santa Fe for a while in the 1930's.

My father used to tell me *La Llorona* dressed like a witch. When I was very small, we owned the house that is now called St. Joseph Hall, where they have meetings. Owls used to gather on the roof, sometimes ten at a time. My dad used to say they were witches. When they came down from the roof, they turned into women dressed in black. You couldn't see their faces. The leader was dressed in white and she was said to be *La Llorona*.

If you called the name "Jesus Christ," or like the *viejitos*— the old people—used to say, "*Jesus, Maria y Jose,*" or if you cried out, "Oh, my God," they would jump back and fly up and then vanish in thin air. Isn't that something? It was very frightening to us.

We moved to California after that and sold the house. When we came back, we lived in a house behind the meeting hall. The people who bought our house are hardly ever there.

We don't see the owls anymore. It's different, now. And the children only believe what they see on the TV.

Margarita Olivas
Mora, NM

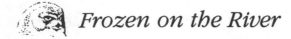 *Frozen on the River*

My dad used to tell me this story when I was growing up here in Las Vegas, New Mexico in the 1950's.

It seems that a woman was married to a man that drank too much—a *borracho*. He would come home late at night from the bar and he would start pushing her around, hitting her and yelling at her. She had two little children and she began to be afraid that he might hurt them.

So, one night, when he was out drinking, she took the children down to the river where Bridge Street is now, and put them under the bridge there. She told them to be quiet and wait for her and that she would return very soon. Then she went home to gather her things and to pack up and leave her husband for good. She had decided that she could not spend another night under the same roof with this man.

Well, it was a very cold night, and she took too long. Who knows why? Maybe she had to feed the horses before she left. Maybe someone came by to visit and she had to pass the time a little bit by sharing some gossip— what we call *platicando*. At any rate, when she finally got back to the bridge, the children had frozen to death.

That was *La Llorona*. To this day, she walks the river bed in Las Vegas, crying and weeping for her children.

Robert V. Montoya
Las Vegas, NM

The Haunting of Pojoaque

When I was nine years old—this was in 1946—we moved from Santa Fe to Pojoaque. My parents weren't religious, so I hadn't gone to church a whole lot, but the whole Pojoaque community in those days was involved in the old church, which was up on the hill by the Pojoaque Pueblo. It's been torn down since then and a new church has been built, but at that time it was an old, old church. A beautiful one, I thought—I could never understand why anyone would want to tear it down. It had an ornate altar painted with the *santos* and the angels—something I had never experienced in my life. When somebody died, we'd go to the funeral there so we didn't have to go to school. That way, we never ditched school, so to speak. All my friends were Spanish. I was the only Anglo.

I don't remember what day it was, but the saint's day that the church was named after was a big day for everyone in the Pojoaque community. There would be a high Mass and a parade, and the priest would have his incense burner and he would sprinkle the ground around the church with holy water. Then a procession would follow, around and around the church, with banners and so on. It was very elaborate and awe-inspiring. The old-timers would have blunderbusses and they'd load them with black powder and shoot them in the air and this smoke would go all over— boom, boom! This would go on all day.

Toward evening, the women would bring food, some of them traveling with horses and wagons, and then the *luminarias* would be lit. The Indians would come, too, since the pueblo was right there. In fact, during the procession around the church, they would beat on drums. It was really, really something. I loved to go because there were so many kids there running around. So when they lit the *luminarias* that night, everyone sat around and started telling stories like: "Don't go into the graveyard at night because the dead people will pull your toes." Or: "If you hear an owl hoot, it means the dead are rising out of their graves."

Anyway, we were running all over the place, the way kids do. Of course, we never went near the cemetery, but we were playing around near the cottonwoods by the river, and an owl started hooting. There were about seven of us kids, and we all stopped to listen to the owl because we thought it was the dead rising. We were very quiet, listening to the owl, when all of a sudden we started hearing some other kind of crying. We looked around, and I'll never forget this: The smoke from the fires had drifted down to the river, the way smoke travels toward a river and settles down in there, and there she was, illuminated in smoke. The lady in black with the veil, and all that. And she was crying, and she walked into the cemetery and then she just walked around in there, crying in a sad and plaintive voice. It scared us terribly, and we took off and ran back to the area where the *luminarias* were, where there was light, and it was then that they told us the story of *La Llorona*.

The story was about a woman named Enriqueta Gomez y Lujan. In the olden days, the Ute Indians had come out of Colorado and taken her twin boys and killed them both down by the river. They had buried them in that cemetery where the church was, and since that time she had been coming there, crying and searching for them among the graves.

Stephen W. Long
Albuquerque, NM

La Llorona Almost Hangs

I was born here in Las Vegas, New Mexico about 78 years ago—on October 12, 1909, in Old Town on the Plaza. My dad came here in 1895 and he built most of this town. It was the best town in New Mexico. It was a wealthy place then, with a lot of gangsters and a lot of sheep and a lot of *frijoles*. This was the shipping center for 300 miles around.

I own the old Kiva Theater here, which was built in 1912—the year New Mexico got its statehood. I bought the theater from my dad's estate in 1930, and then I refurbished it completely. They used to have vaudeville shows there in the very early days. Later on, we began showing Spanish movies and westerns. We had it rented to one of the biggest movie companies in Hollywood back then. In fact, Tom Mix and a lot of the big stars of that day would appear on the stage in person. There was always a packed house—the admission was 10 cents.

I've got the theater on the market now for $150,000—that's negotiable, though. The marquee itself is the original one, as a matter of fact; it's very beautiful. We've got an electric folding ticket machine, and 275 upholstered chairs—some of them are the real fancy opera seats. And there's a new roof, an RCA sound system, and some very up-to-date equipment. It has the original oak floors; you don't find theaters like that anymore.

Does it sound like I'm trying to sell it to you? Well, I am. There's only one other theater in town, and Las Vegas has 16,000 people who love to go to the movies, and it's growing like gangbusters because this is a beautiful place to live, very peaceful and slow-paced. A perfect place to move and buy a movie theater with a lot of historical value! So if you're interested, I'm in the telephone book.

Well, I'm supposed to tell you a *La Llorona* tale, so here it is.

There was a story floating around when I was growing up here, supposedly about *La Llorona*, that she shot a fellow in the heart and the judge sentenced her to die by hanging. So they took her to an area five miles north of here called *El Barrio de Los Ortegas*, by the Montezuma Castle. They put the noose around her neck and nobody would pull the rope, I guess because they figured she'd haunt them after she died or some such thing. So they told her, "You can go free," and they let her go on the spot.

Frank Maloof
Las Vegas, NM

The 'R' Car to Tortilla Flats

I lived in East Los Angeles during the 1940's—on South Fresno Street, to be exact, right across from the "White Fence" area—so I consider myself to be a bit knowledgeable about the *pachuco* era. It is believed that the term *pachuco* originated from the word *pocho*, which refers to a native-born Californian of Spanish descent.

The *pachuco* style of dress was very distinctive, and grooming was fastidious. The cuffs on the pants were called "ankle chokers." The pants were very baggy—in fact, at the knees, the material was almost three yards wide. They were "Dutch pressed" into two pleats, one in the front and one on the side. The shoes, which were highly polished wingtips, had soles nearly two inches thick. Of course, the hair was greased into an elaborate ducktail—much classier than Elvis Presley's. Some *pachucos* also had an "inaugural" cross tattooed on their foreheads between the eyebrows, while others had the cross on their right hand between the thumb and index finger. In later years, I had a rose tattooed over the cross on my hand. My cousin Bobby had the cross on his forehead professionally removed by a doctor.

The Anglos and Blacks used to imitate the *pachuco* style of dress. They called themselves "Zoot Suiters." The most popular material for these suits was sharkskin, which was shiny and looked very classy.

My stepfather hated this style of dress. He used to take my shoes to the shoe repair shop and have the soles removed, and a few weeks later I'd just go back and have new ones nailed on. It was a constant tug of war between us. I wasn't the only one, though—a lot of the *plebe*—the other guys—had the same problem with their dads.

The Hispanics (as they call us now) of East Los Angeles, like the Hispanics everywhere else, all knew about *La Llorona*. Richard Morales and his little brother "Nacho" claim that they used to see her almost every Friday night, usually about 15 or 20 minutes past midnight, after they left the late show at the Crystal Movie Theater on Whittier Boulevard. They would see her riding the "R" car, which was a trolley that ran up 7th on Whittier to Indiana Street. She always seemed to be sitting alone in the back of the trolley car, so the story goes, and it was easy to spot her because the inside of the trolley was extremely well lit. They insisted it was *La Llorona* because she always appeared in the same car at the same time, every Friday night like clockwork, and some people who saw her claimed that she would suddenly vaporize.

David Gonzales, a friend of mine who tried to be a *pachuco* but could never really carry it off because his dad was too strict, said that he spotted *La Llorona* walking on South Fresno Street toward Euclid Avenue one Friday evening. Many of the *pachucos* of that day were constantly looking for her, checking out 38th Street, *La Washington*, California Street, the whole city, in fact. I have to admit, though, that I never saw her myself.

The old-timers used to see her a lot more often. They said it was because they were believers, while us younger kids were not.

Edward Garcia Kraul
Santa Fe, NM

The Horse That Left No Tracks

La Llorona used to haunt the travelers coming into the La Joya and Pecos areas from Rowe back in the 1870's. My *visabuelo*—my great grandfather—told me the following story of his experience in those days:

"We were on the way to Santa Fe in the old covered wagon, and it was a little before dusk when we arrived in the La Joya area. I was traveling with your father and your great grandmother (my wife, Ramoncita). It was early summer and there had been a sudden and heavy rain. The air was still damp and smelled very beautiful. The *cedros*—the juniper trees—were still glistening with the raindrops and the air was so clear you could see the pale gold of the *muerdago,* what you call mistletoe, in the distance.

"We had stopped for a few minutes to eat some food we had brought with us, when we saw in the distance a lady riding a white horse with her *tapalo*—her shawl—floating behind her. She was galloping very fast and coming directly toward us. We thought of the story of 'La Llorona on the white horse,' which was very popular at that time, and chills ran up my spine. I told your father and my Ramoncita, 'Let's get inside the wagon and close the flaps until she goes by.' We threw our food into the back and climbed in as quickly as we could. The flaps were not very good; they were tattered and frayed from the weather and we had to hold them closed.

"As we huddled inside, we heard her approach, dismount, and walk around the wagon as though she was inspecting it. We were very frightened. You might wonder why we would be frightened of a woman on a horse, but there was something that was not natural about her, as though she came from another world—*un aparacion de el otro mundo.* Then we heard her mount her horse and ride off. We still waited a long time before we decided that it was safe to look out. To us it seemed like forever! We climbed out of the wagon and, upon looking around, we saw her footprints, but for all the searching we did we could not find the hoofprints of the horse. We walked for quite a distance in search of some disturbance in the sand, some sign of prints, but we saw nothing at all. The sand was still wet and untouched after the storm.

"There are people that claim she was a very beautiful woman with jet black hair and a very suntanned complexion."

Carlos Valdez
Espanola, NM

The Test Drive

I was a miner in the 1930's and was living in Raton around that time. In those days, nearly everyone in town was involved in the coal mining operations of the area in one way or the other. There wasn't much of a reason to live there unless you mined or maybe raised a little cattle.

I used to spend many hours in the *cantinas*—the bars — those were rough days and we used to swap a lot of stories to pass the time. There was this bartender, Romero, who told me this story and even as I tell it to you now, it gives me the willies.

Seems that this fella placed an ad in the Raton Range, I believe it was, during the years of the Great Depression, to sell his Model T car for $100. The advertisement ran a long time and there were no takers until one hot summer day when a woman called and expressed a real interest in seeing his car and taking it for a test drive. This was unusual—a woman calling a man to make a business transaction of that sort in those days, but the little lady sounded real determined and he sure as hell needed the money.

So he arranged to meet her down by the railroad yards at 7:30 that evening, and when he got there, a woman in a black, heavy cloak was waiting for him. The sun was about to set but it was still very, very warm and there she was, dressed for winter. She indicated to him that she would crank the car up, and after she did, she motioned for him to move over to the passenger's side so she could drive. Then she hopped in like she really knew her business and took off like a bat out of hell, if you'll excuse the expression. They were going very fast on the dirt road, 20 or 25 miles an hour, and after about 10 minutes or so of this, he turned to her and asked, "Lady, just where do you think you're going? This is just a test drive." She didn't answer him. He even mentioned to her that he was starting to feel a little green around the gills with all the bouncing around, but he may as well have been talking to himself for all the response he got.

After a time, the car began to get very cold inside, and then the sun set, and still they kept going. It was like a dream, almost, where a person has no sense of time or place. A few times he wanted to just holler, "Stop the car," or throw the door open and jump out, but he couldn't do nothing but stare like a zombie through the windshield like he was paralyzed. And the car was getting colder and colder inside.

Now, this fella was also a veteran of the trenches in World War I and so he had a good sense of survival. He knew there was something real peculiar happening, and he decided to just sit tight and be quiet and not fight this feeling that had come over him of being paralyzed. He figured to himself that if he got out of this situation in one piece, he'd buy everybody back at the bar a drink or two.

Anyway, the road started to get a lot rougher and they were bouncing around like a couple of Mexican jumping beans on a hot plate. Finally, it seemed like they hit sand and then they were going down a hill of sorts. The sand got deeper and deeper, and the car began to get bogged down, and then the wheels started spinning and pretty soon they stopped turning completely. So they just sat there for a while. It was deadly quiet outside as well as inside. No crickets, no frogs, no coyotes, no nothing. You could have heard an egg frying at a hundred yards.

After about an eternity or so, the lady turned to this fella for the first time and in this deep, watery voice that seemed to come from the bottom of a well, she snarled, "I'll take the car. You get out. *Now!*" Then she pushed one of those little Bull Durham tobacco bags into his hands. It was full of coins, but they felt more like ice cubes. At that exact second, his strength shot back into his body and he threw the car door open and ran as fast as he could into the night. As he was running from the river bed, scrambling up the sandy sides of the arroyo, he could hear her voice follow him, rising into a blood-curdling wail that echoed everywhere.

He got a ride with some people back to Raton. They told him that he wasn't far from the town of Chico. After he described the woman to various folks in the course of the next few days, someone said to him, "That's *La Llorona*. She goes down to that particular river bed a lot. That's the first time, though, that she's used a car to get there." This fella supposedly moved out of Raton right after that incident and settled in San Antonio.

Waylon Tuttle
Tulsa, OK

The Haunting of Placita Rafaela

My name is Phillip Griego. I'm on the Santa Fe City Council and I'm also a partner with Lawyers Title Company.

The story goes that a Mr. Garcia decided to visit Paul's Lounge here in Santa Fe one Good Friday, even though his wife begged him not to because she was afraid he would be cursed for it. He went anyway, and drank there all day long. By the time he left that night, he was pretty well inebriated. He started walking home through Tenorio Street, and as he neared Garcia Street, right where Acequia Madre turns, he heard someone crying. He turned and saw a woman shrouded completely in white, standing in the moonlight and pointing at him. Terrified, he ran up the Acequia Madre to the front of Tito's Market, my dad's grocery store, and tripped and fell down there in the street. By the time he got up and dusted himself off, she was gone.

As he turned down Placita Rafaela, he saw a little baby lying in the middle of his driveway, wrapped in a white blanket and crying pitifully. He walked over and picked it up, wondering whose baby this was and why it was there in the middle of the night. Noticing that its face was covered with the blanket, he opened it to look and there she was, a baby-sized *La Llorona*, staring at him with her big, dark, penetrating eyes and her sharp white teeth and her big, ugly, bony hand pointing at him. He dropped the bundle and ran into the house, and he hasn't had a drink since that night.

Phil Griego
Santa Fe, NM

Ralph Martinez' Long Ride Home

My family has been in the Santa Fe area for more than 150 years. My father, Abel Dominguez, was from Tesuque, born in 1894, and my grandpa used to own the Bishops Lodge properties.

In 1949, Ralph Martinez was a projectionist at the Paris Theater, which was on San Francisco Street two blocks from where the Lensic Theater is now. One night, he was riding his bike home after running the movie projector through a double horror feature—I remember one of the movies was "Frankenstein Meets the Wolf Man," and I can't remember the other one, but I know it was a Dracula movie—and he came upon a lady on Magdalena Lane who was only about three or four feet tall, with scraggly hair. She started this terrible moaning and crying as soon as she saw him, wringing her hands and wailing something terrible in this high-pitched, deafening scream. She had a wrinkly little face and a long ugly nose covered with little warts.

It scared the pants off Ralph, so he just dropped his bike on the spot and ran to the Visarraga home, where they let him spend the rest of the night. The next day, he took a bunch of us guys to go get his bike. We found it on the side of the road, right where he said he had left it. To the day he died, Ralph swore up and down it was *La Llorona*.

Juan Dominguez
Santa Fe, NM

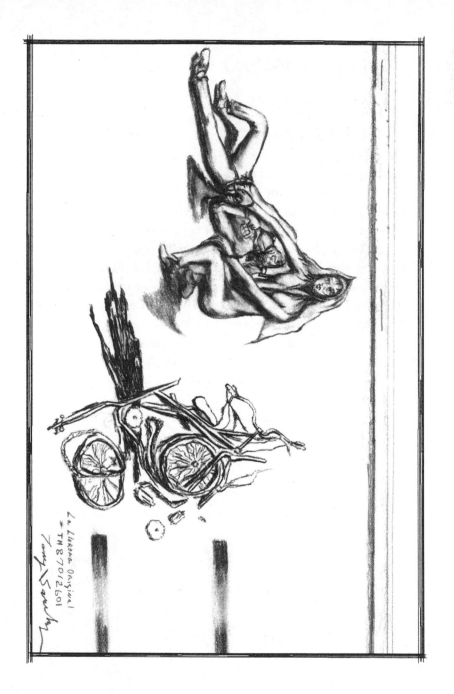

La Llorona Original
TN8701/2601
Tony Sancho

33

 *El Molino*

In 1925 here in Santa Fe, where Sosaya Lane meets Acequia Madre, our *primo*—our cousin—Ramon Vigil had a *molenito* — a small mill—and he used to grind the corn for the people. Every ten sacks he ground for you, you had to give him one sack in payment. The wheels of the mill were constantly turning. He was very, very busy. People ate a lot of corn tortillas in those days.

At night, if you walked by the mill, you could hear the creaking and groaning of the wheels, and we used to get the chills listening to it. It was said that *La Llorona* would appear and that her crying would mingle with the noise of the wheels grinding the corn late at night. You wouldn't know it was her, though, until you were practically standing next to her. My *primo* said that he ran into her one night and she had skin like leather and her eyes glowed in the dark, like a cat, but were reddish in color.

When us kids walked by the mill at night, we would say a whole rosary in just a half a block!

Alfonso "Trompo" Trujillo
Santa Fe, NM

The Llorona

My name is Mel Apodaca, and I am on the County Commission in Santa Fe.

The first time I ever heard of the *Llorona*, I think I was six or seven years of age. My grandmother on my father's side of the family would threaten to let the *Llorona* take me away while I was asleep if I didn't behave. She told me that the *Llorona* was a lady that had lost her baby as a result of drowning and that she had gone out of her mind as a result. So the *Llorona* would go out at night when other women's babies were asleep, and she would steal them from their cribs or beds and take them to the river and drown them—especially if those babies did not behave or cried a lot.

According to my grandma, the *Llorona* was always crying and making hysterical sounds of agony and that this was how I could tell when she was coming for me. She also would tell me that if I didn't stop crying and go to sleep, the *Llorona* would know where I was. Needless to say, it worked every time.

All this was told to me in Spanish as my grandma didn't speak English.

Melisendro Apodaca
Arroyo Seco, NM

The Sheepherder
Takes a Bath

My dad used to tell us this story that his grandfather had told him about one of the uncles in our family.

My family lived in Roy, New Mexico, where we used to have sheep that grazed in Ocate. During the time that the *gringos* were having their Civil War, about 1865, this brother of my great grandfather, Ramon Sanchez, never liked to take a bath from the time he had been a little *niño*. And he was always told that one of these days *La Llorona* was going to grab him and give him a good scrubbing. Ramon loved to be out there with the sheep in Ocate while they grazed. One day, one of the great grandmas went to the great grandpa, Juan Jose, who was the sheep owner, and told him, "You have to force Ramon to take a bath because we just can't stand the way he smells anymore. We have to sit and eat close to him and sometimes we have to chase him away so we can finish our food."

The *patron* went to talk to Ramon and they had a few words. That evening, they saw Ramon gathering wood and warming water near a hidden cove in the arroyo, around where the sheep grazed. Some of the family went to spy on him to see if he would really take a bath, and they watched him fill this wooden *cajete* —a tub—with hot water and then get in. After a while, they got tired of watching him and went in to finish the chores.

After they finished the chores, they all went outside because it was a warm evening and the moon was out. A long time passed until someone said, "Where is Ramon? It has been a very long time now since he went to take his bath." A couple of the old-timers decided to investigate and they went down to the arroyo and there he was, still sitting in the tub, scrubbing and scrubbing.

Emilio, one of the old-timers, said to him, "Do you realize you've been in here half the night? Everyone is getting ready to go to sleep." Well, Ramon looked like he had seen a ghost. He kept scrubbing and scrubbing and he said to Emilio, "A woman came here and sat down right here, next to the *cajete*, and she told me that she would scrub the hide off my back if I didn't take a bath every week." Well, they had to force him to get out of there. He was wrinkled up like a raisin.

Later on, they said it was *La Llorona* who visited Ramon that night, because she was dressed in black, very beautiful, quite young, and she whimpered in this very low cry while she talked. The important thing, though, is that Ramon took a bath every week from that day on until he died of old age about 65 years later.

Irene Ortiz
Santa Fe, NM

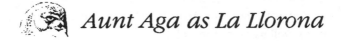

Aunt Aga as La Llorona

Placita Rafaela is a cul-de-sac off the Acequia Madre, about 300 feet from the intersection of Arroyo Tenorio, Garcia Street and East Manhattan, and is a *barrio* where a branch of the Garcia family has lived for many generations.

Ageda Garcia, wife of Epifanio Garcia, was the matriarch of the whole clan—not just of her own children, but her grandchildren, great grandchildren, and all of the other relatives who lived in that compound. She even had authority over the animals, of which she owned four or five dogs and at least three cats. Epifanio was a hard-working man who was employed for more than 50 years at the Boyle greenhouses, along with his son, Alfonso, his nephews, and his grand nephews.

One evening, after Ageda (or "Tia Aga" as she was called by everyone) had worked hard all day, she went outside to call her son Alfonso and two of her nephews, Roberto and John, because it was their bedtime. After considerable hollering for the young boys to come in the house, she finally gave up trying. It was a beautiful spring evening and the aroma of the lilacs was everywhere—there was a feeling of summer in the air and many people were still outside.

Anyway, Tia Aga hit on the idea of climbing on some stilts and wrapping herself in a white sheet in an effort to convince the boys that she was *La Llorona* and that they had definitely better get into the house without fail! She figured that this method of threatening the little ones with an appearance by *La Llorona* would probably work, since nearly everyone was afraid of running into *La Llorona* because the compound was right off the acequia. Besides, Tia Aga was that kind of a person—she had a wonderful sense of humor and that is why everyone loved her so much. The fact that she cussed like a sailor didn't matter to anyone. She was the boss and commanded respect from the relatives as well as all of the neighbors.

Sneaking around the back of the house, she caught the boys by surprise. It was dark already, and all they could see was this terrifying creature, about seven or eight feet tall, coming toward them in a white shroud. As soon as she realized she had their attention, she started to whimper and wail in the same voice that everyone had heard from the real *La Llorona* at one time or another. She knew it was a very convincing performance, because she heard them gasp with fear and surprise and then scramble to get away from her. She felt gratified at her acting ability and thought to herself: "Good. I can use this every time these boys act up." But what happened was that John Martinez, a very mischievous boy who was playing with the others, ran up to examine *La Llorona* and, in his enthusiasm, he tripped Tia Aga and knocked her off her stilts, and she fell flat on her bottom.

The Garcia family will long remember Tia Aga as *La Llorona!*

Margie Ulibarri
Santa Fe, NM

La Llorona Gets Shot

I was born in 1906 in a very old adobe house—it was considered old even then—on my dad's ranch, which was right on the river in the El Macho area of Pecos, New Mexico. My mother was Rosita Gallegos; my father, Agapito Cortez. I worked in the mines for 27 years, both hard rock and coal mines in Madrid and Santa Rita, New Mexico, and in Montana, Idaho, and Washington. After that, I went to work in the Chicago Post Office. I've got black lung now, and I have to have oxygen. I have a sign on my door that says: "Lungs At Work: No Smoking." Believe it or not, if I didn't have it there, some people wouldn't think twice about lighting a cigarette in my living room. You could blow up the whole place, you know.

My dad was a mail carrier in Pecos, and he delivered the mail on horseback. He always carried a .44 pistol. You never knew in those days what you might run into.

In 1904, there was a terrible flood in Pecos that washed away many houses and some bridges. It lasted for several days and many people had to leave their houses and stay with families who were lucky enough not to live so close to the river.

My father was delivering the mail during this time in an area called Penasco Alto, which means "high rocky place," right above Juanita Byrd's ranch in a neighborhood called Encinoso. They called it that because it was full of oak trees. Now it's called the Hidden Valley Ranch. It is a very beautiful spot. *La Llorona* used to cry and wail around there. People heard her many times; they said she was a phantom dressed in black who wandered among the rocks and junipers.

One winter night after the flooding began, my father was traveling through that area on his horse when he heard the terrible wailing and crying of *La Llorona*. It was so close, perhaps no more than 10 or 15 feet away, that he got his .44 out and fired it toward the source of the sound. The blood-curdling cries stopped almost immediately, and no one ever heard the sound of *La Llorona* again in that particular spot.

My relations, Guadalupe and Porfiria Gonzales, used to tell this story to many others. It was one of the first stories I heard as a child. More than 80 years have passed and I still remember it very well.

Victor Cortez
Santa Fe, NM

Mourning at Rosario Cemetery

On an early summer evening in 1943, I was playing on Jimenez Street near the Arroyo Mascarenas here in Santa Fe with my friend Mary Alice Moya. It was about 7:30 or 8:00 when Mary said to me, "Look over to the other side of the arroyo." I looked over there and I saw an old woman dressed in black with a *tapalo*—a shawl—over her head. Every three or four steps she took, she would raise her head and cry very low. Then she would lower her head like she was praying, and take another few steps.

She was heading toward the Rosario Cemetery, from where the DeVargas Mall is now. My aunt Josefita Martinez, who is 86, and my uncle Luis Martinez, who is 84, said they used to see an old woman walking late in the evenings toward the Rosario Cemetery where the Rosario Chapel is.

A lot of people would say that it was *La Llorona* checking on the people who had died. They only would see her when someone had just been buried.

Irene Ortiz
Santa Fe, NM

 # Ramon Garcia's Last Date

Around 1925, this man, Ramon Garcia, used to go out with different women. His wife wasn't the jealous type, but she was very religious and she didn't want him to be stepping out and all that jazz, you know? She said to him one time, "If you go out tonight, something's going to happen to you—you're going to meet up with the wrong party." He thought to himself, "She doesn't know what she's talking about."

So he went downtown to this bar called *La Rendija* —"The Crack"—and he had a couple of drinks. He danced a while and it got to be about 2:00 in the morning, so he started walking home. Right where Canyon Road meets Garcia Street, he spotted this woman walking in front of him. She was very attractive, very enticing. He was maybe 20 or 30 feet behind her, so he decided to walk a little faster.

When he finally caught up to her, he saw that she was wearing a heavy veil over her face. So he lifted the veil to see her better, and to maybe give her a kiss, and as soon as he did that, he realized that he was looking right into the face of *La Llorona*. With the rays of the moon shining on her face, she looked like a skeleton.

Ramon Garcia never stepped out on his wife again. He died not too long ago, and he said that he would never forget this experience.

Fred "El Gallina" Montoya
Santa Fe, NM

The Road from Puerta de Luna

I do carpentry and other work for my cousin, Louie Montoya, who owns Latin Styles here in Albuquerque. It's a real nice little store that sells T-shirts, windbreakers, magazines, and stuff for low riders like mad dog sunglasses. Louie's an editor for Low Rider Magazine, which is published in California and sells 100,000 copies every month.

Now that I'm finished giving a little endorsement for my *primo's* business, I would like to tell of a terrible experience I had with *La Llorona* and how it changed my life for the better.

About four years ago on the Fourth of July, I decided to walk the road from Puerta de Luna to the Nuestra Senora del Refugio Church in Santa Rosa, which I think is about six miles—maybe more. This is the same area, by the way, where there was a big shoot-out with Billy the Kid once—in fact, there are bullet holes in one of the buildings there. Anyway, the church was having its centennial and there had been celebrations going on for most of the day. Unfortunately, I got started late, but I decided to try and make it anyway before it got too dark out. Little did I know that something would happen to me on the road that would make me get there faster than I ever thought was possible.

I had gone about two miles and I was saying my rosary as I walked along, trying to say it with a feeling of sincerity because I was doing penance, and also trying to hurry a little bit because it was already starting to get dark. I was approaching this little bridge where the road turns very sharply to the right, when I heard what I thought was a wolf howling from a *bosque*—a patch of woods—off to the right and up ahead of me. It was a very sad kind of howling, very drawn out but real loud, but as it faded it began to sound more like the cry of a woman. At that moment, I knew I was hearing the sound of *La Llorona,* because this was the same area of the river where others had heard her. As I tell you this story, I feel the same fear I felt then. I can't describe to you how surprised and frightened I was because there was no one around—everyone was at the church and the few houses I had passed along the road were dark and deserted.

Right then and there, I began to say my rosary as loudly as I could: "Holy Mary, Mother of God, pray for us sinners now and at the hour of our death, Amen." And I said it louder and louder as I approached the bridge that went over the little river that separated me from the *bosque* and *La Llorona.* As I moved toward the bridge, I could feel myself starting to sweat. My heart was pounding and my legs felt shaky and weak as I imagined her suddenly stepping out and confronting me in the road. I knew that I still had a long way to go and that there was no turning back; it was like this was a test for me.

After I finally got across the little bridge, I ran all the rest of the way, hollering my rosary as loud as I could to try to drown out the sound of the howling that seemed to be right behind me. When I got to the church, I fell to my knees and realized I had reached the last bead. At that moment, I understood that my faith was stronger than ever, and it still is. I know that will never change. So for that reason, I feel that God put *La Llorona* in my path to strengthen my belief in Him.

Ernest Lucero
Albuquerque, NM

El Borracho on the
Santa Fe River

They call me *El Enano*—"The Dwarf"—and I am 64 years old, now. I have lived in Santa Fe all my life except when I was in World War II—the Big One.

Platicava Papa—Dad used to tell us—of an incident that occurred when *El Gallina*, Manuel Montoya (brother of Louie, Fred, and Dickie Montoya), was Chief of Police in Santa Fe in the 1940's. He was a good man. *Les comprava provisiones a los pobres*—he would buy groceries for the poor—out of his own pocket during Christmas. And he would provide a little "hair of the dog" to *los borrachos*—the winos—when they had hang-overs. Everybody liked and respected *El Gallina*.

There on Lopez Street lived a *borracho* and his name was Juan de Dios Lopez. I use this name and not his real one so as not to insult his family. One night, the Chief was driving a police car on Alto Street near Closson Street and some people ran to him as he was driving by and said that someone was drowning in the Santa Fe River. So *El Gallina* got out and looked, and there was Juan de Dios Lopez struggling in the water, crying for assistance. These other people, I guess they couldn't swim. So *El Gallina* jumped into the river and saved this poor soul who was crying for his life.

Juan had been beat up and his nose was bleeding very bad. He was white as sheet, ready to pass out. The Chief took him home and Juan told him that *La Llorona* had beat him up! And that she said to him, "*Si te vuelvo a ver pedo, te vuelvo a golpear*— If I see you drunk again, I will beat you up again."

This happened to Juan when he was about 25 years old, I think, and I know he lived to be at least 100, so he had 75 years

of being sober because after *La Llorona* beat him up that night, he never had another drink. And with the money he saved from not drinking, he built his family a very fine home on Calle Lopez.

El Enano
Santa Fe, NM

El Rancho de Los Maranos

People call me "Bushman" because I do landscaping for the movie companies—I'm the person who takes care of the vegetation, like trimming the shrubbery, etc. And I have a barbershop here in Albuquerque, so if I'm not cutting bushes, I'm cutting hair.

In 1943, when I was seven, I moved to East Grand Plains, New Mexico, a little farming community about 12 miles east of Roswell, to spend time with my Uncle Rumaldo, who practically raised me. The rest of my family was in Roswell, opening up a business at the arcade there. One of the ranch-farms in East Grand Plains was named *"El Rancho de Los Maranos"*—"Pig Ranch"—which dates back back to the early 1800's and sits in the path of the Chisholm Trail. Now it's called "Oasis Ranch," which I guess they changed to make it sound a little better.

My uncle was a field foreman on this ranch and he used to tell me that *La Llorona* traveled through the Hondo Valley into Roswell, and out to *"El Rancho de Los Maranos."* This particular ranch had its own jailhouse, which they used in the earlier days, and its own company store. Sometimes, there could be as many as 100 or 150 people living at the *campo*, which is what they called the living quarters. *La Llorona* was supposed to have appeared on several occasions at the south end of the ranch in an area full of big cottonwood trees—what we call *alamos*—where the irrigation ditches were. When there was such a sighting, word would spread quickly throughout the *campo*. She'd float among the trees in the dusk wearing a white cloak, moaning and screaming and scaring everybody half out of their minds. Since I worked on this ranch off and on for a number of years, I naturally became a real believer in *La Llorona*. It was impossible not to believe in her because of all of the people who said they had seen her.

When I was 11, I had to move from the ranch to East Los Angeles. In the period I was there, I met all kinds of people from New Mexico, and all of them were very well acquainted with *La Llorona*—they had seen her in places such as Deming, Silver City, and a lot of the smaller towns down south. At that age, I believed that she was a native of New Mexico. It never occurred to me that she might pop up somewhere else. So you can imagine how surprised I was to learn that she made regular appearances in a place called Coyote Pass in East L.A. There had been a gang killing there and the place had a real bad reputation that dated back many years. You could take your family there for a picnic during the day, but at night Coyote Pass was transformed into a dangerous jungle of sinful activity where the kidnapped, robbed, and murdered were dumped under the cover of night.

When I was 15, I moved back to *"El Rancho de Los Maranos"* and was put in charge of irrigating the ranch at the south end, which you may recall is the exact spot where *La Llorona* made her appearances. My uncle also told me that I was to do this work at night! Word spread very fast throughout the *campo* and soon my best friend Santos was making jokes that I should take a crucifix and flash it in her face if she appeared. Santos wasn't afraid of anything—in fact, his dad had been in Pancho Villa's army. I was more excited than scared, if you want to know the truth.

As it turned out, it was one of the roughest nights I had ever experienced as an irrigator. The ditch busted three times, the planted cotton broke up all night long, and the fields were getting so much water that the cotton that had grown out was pretty much destroyed. I spent the whole night shoveling in a high wind and trying to secure the ditch caps, and I forgot all about *La Llorona*. I guess I thought to myself, "Only a fool would come out on a night like this."

At six o'clock in the morning, my uncle showed up with my replacement and the first thing he said when he got down from his pickup was, "Well, did you see her?" I said to him, "No, just a lot of wind." Later on, though, I thought to myself that maybe she had appeared by one of the trees and watched me work through the night. Could it have been *La Llorona* who made it such a difficult night for me?

Isidro Guerrero
Albuquerque, NM

 *Great Balls of Fire*

A section of what used to be the Old Santa Fe Trail was changed to "College Street" during the days of St. Michael's College. *Los Corchos de La Calle de El Colegio*—The "Corks" from College Street—tell of *las pelotas de lumbre y La Llorona*— the balls of fire and *La Llorona*.

The Corks were a gang of guys from Santa Fe who used to hang around together in the 1940's. They got that name because they drank wine—you know, wine bottles in those days didn't have screw tops like some of them do now.

One of these *Corchos*, Dickie Archuleta, was going towards La Calle Tenorio through College Street when he met up with Salvador Tucker. Salvie was coming from downtown and had taken a short cut through the area near the oldest house on East DeVargas Street by the Boyle Greenhouse, and had cut across the old *camposanto*—cemetery grounds—which is the present location of the Public Employees Retirement Association (PERA) Building where the State workers are employed now.

I understand that when the local politicians decided to build the PERA Building on Catholic cemetery property, they unceremoniously dug up the bodies and, in cahoots with certain church officials, buried them somewhere else. There are a lot of people still living today who had family members dug up this way. When you think about it, it was a terrible thing to do to the families of these poor people, if that is what really happened.

It is said that *La Llorona* turns the lights on and off in the PERA Building to this day. In fact, many of the office workers have seen her in broad daylight, and the cleaning crews hear her slamming doors and crying in the night. When she is seen, she is usually walking down one of the hallways, all in black, and as she walks, she slowly fades into nothing. Other times, people can hear her feet on the back stairs or hallways, but she is invisible. She has even thrown someone down the stairs. But that's another story.

Anyway, getting back to the *Corchos*, Dickie claims to this day that after he and Salvie crossed the *camposanto* and then headed down Manhattan and up College Street, *La Llorona* was right behind them throwing big balls of fire up the street toward Camino de Las Animas—which means, as you may already know, "Street of the Spirits."

Demetrio Lujan
Pueblo, CO

The Courtyard Fantasy

I come from the Tates who founded the village of Taterville,
near San Jose and San Juan in San Miguel County, New Mexico.
I come from a family of artists. You might have known my late
brother, Bill, who had a gallery on Canyon Road in Santa Fe for
many years. I like to write books, myself.

I designed and built Emilio's Restaurant here in Espanola.
The chile they serve is out of this world, no question about it. If
you've never been inside, it has a real authentic "Wild West"
motif, with swinging doors like in a saloon and little booths that
look like the inside of a stagecoach. People think those are real
bullet holes in the walls, but the truth of the matter is, I ended up
getting out my drill, turning it on, and running full speed ahead
into the walls with the thing going full blast. I'd had a few beers
and it seemed like a good idea at the time.

I ran away from home back in Tulsa when I was 14 and rode
just about every railroad line in this country and visited every
state by the time I was 20—I figure I traveled close to a quarter of
a million miles either by freight or by thumb. I've got a lot of
stories to tell as a result of my travels, but one of my favorites is
that of the infamous and horrible *La Llorona,* the weeping
woman, who strikes terror into the hearts of the innocent and
leaves the guilty quivering in fear for their very souls.

Legend has it that this ghost woman we know as *La Llorona*
travels at night from place to place, sometimes on a white horse
and sometimes on a black horse.

She is torn between good and bad—in other words, between
Satan the Devil and God. Her soul or spirit is never at rest. She
cries out at night in a sound of complete terror to please help her
put her soul to rest.

Many of the New Mexico old-timers claim, in fact, that they

have seen her setting on her horse in very remote places in northern New Mexico, mainly around rivers, streams, creeks, and even dry arroyos, in her white robe, swinging a sword or whip and screeching very loud in a blood-curdling sound for you to follow her and she would lead you from the Devil and back to the Church. This was the good side of her spirit. On the bad side, she might curse and ask for you to follow her to Hell, where she felt her soul may be resting. In short, her soul was lost and she was seeking same—it was in Heaven or Hell.

Many people say she did scare a heck of a lot of folks back to going to church, and scared the little kids into being good.

I have a friend named Dennis who was born in Dixon, New Mexico. He is now 55 years of age, and he will swear he saw *La Llorona* when he was about nine or ten years old. His house was in a courtyard completely surrounded by an eight-foot wall, with a gate at one end. One day, someone forgot to put the chain around the post to lock the gate, and in she came, into the courtyard on her white stallion, and then stopped at his house, where he and his two brothers and sister were playing marbles on the flagstone in the front. She never made a sound—just stood there for a couple of minutes. Then she rode away very fast, out the gate and into the dark.

Dennis said it scared them so bad that they never went out of the house for two days and boy, were they good little boys and girls!!

George O. Tate
Espanola, NM

Terrorizing Las Colonias

I would like to tell of an incident that happened to a group of people in April, 1954. At that time, I was 15, and my husband, Alfonso, my brother-in-law Jose, and my cousin Isidro had traveled from Las Vegas, New Mexico to Avondale, Colorado, near Pueblo, to work in the fields. There were some houses that were loaned to the workers there. The house we stayed in was a very long one, and there were three or four families staying in it.

Around 12:30 one morning, we heard a loud noise, a terrible wailing sound, coming from the river about a half a mile away. It woke everyone up, not just in our house, but in all of the surrounding houses. We ran outside and the cry was as loud as could be and it seemed very close. All of us knew right away it was *La Llorona*.

Alfonso and some other men decided to get in the car and investigate. The car had spotlights—the kind you used then to blind the deer. The ones who stayed behind could see them with the spotlight when they got to the river.

The crying continued. It was so loud that it made our ears ring. Well, what happened was that they heard the cry coming from the other side of the river, so they drove around to get to the other side through a shallow area in the water, and as soon as they got there, the sound of the crying would then seem to be coming from the opposite side. So they would have to cross the river again. This happened about four times, I think. Maybe more. Then it stopped as suddenly as it had started.

We lived there in the *colonias*—the settlement—for three months. There was a little chapel there, but they never held Mass. See, these *colonias* were away from the town; they were for people working in the fields. There was a cemetery next to the chapel. On the night *La Llorona* came to the river, there was a sound from around this little chapel. You know the sound of a football game, when you're in a very big group of people, and it sounds like the buzzing of bees? This is the sound that came from the chapel in the pitch black night that she came. The buzzing lasted almost a half hour, and then it all stopped.

The next day, we went to the chapel to see if there was anything unusual there, but there was no sign of anything.

Joann Baca
Santa Fe, NM

La Lloron Original

El Dia de San Geronimo y
La Noche de La Llorona

This is a story entitled "The Day of Saint Jerome and the Night of the Weeping Woman." It was told to me by a fellow who died about 20 years ago, when he was 78. I will not mention his name because his widow is still alive and so are his six children and many grandchildren.

In the early 1920's, this fellow had a white horse that he used to ride around, a real nice looking horse. One night, there was a big dance in the village of Agua Fria to celebrate the Festival of San Geronimo. Well, this fellow's father told him not to go to the dance and especially not to take that particular horse, since it would get tired. See, the horse had been worked heavily that day in the fields and the village was a good five or six miles down the road. Just to make sure that his son wouldn't go, the father said to him, "I'll put a curse on you—if you go out, something bad will happen to you." The guy said to himself, "My dad's old-fashioned. An old timer."

And so off he went on the white horse, which was called Blanco. About midnight, he decided to start home from the dance. He would have stayed longer, but it was getting cloudy and there was only a half moon. Right around where they have the farmer's market now every summer, across the Santa Fe River on Alameda Street, he spotted something moving around on the ground right near the front of his dad's house. He couldn't see too good because it was dark, first of all, and second of all, this thing was in the rabbit bushes. (That's what we called the *chamiso* because the rabbits used to hide in it when we hunted them.)

So he got off Blanco and walked over to this thing, which looked in the dark like an animal of some kind. It was just lying there and not moving, and when he reached down and touched it, he could feel clothing. So he figured then that it was a person. He realized that it was lying face down, so he rolled it over and then he could see that it was a woman, about four feet tall. At that exact moment, the half moon came out from under a cloud and he saw that this woman had a beak, like a bird. She (or maybe I should say "it") started wailing, and he recognized the sound right away because he had heard *La Llorona* at night by the river, and now here he was looking right into her terrible face.

He let go of this thing and ran into the house. He told his dad about it and his dad said to him, "So the curse came true."

Fred "El Gallina" Montoya
Santa Fe, NM

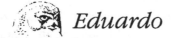 *Eduardo*

On that cold fall evening he first heard *La Llorona,* Eduardo had just finished sweeping the long marble hallway in the PERA Building and had met his wife downstairs at the main doors to pick up the dinner she had prepared. She kissed him and reminded him to bring home the dishes at the end of his shift; he always seemed to forget. He returned inside the building, past the high, fresco-covered walls, down the stairwell to his niche. There, on his stool in front of the heater, he unwrapped the fresh-roasted chile, still-warm tortillas and the little foil package of *chicharones,* and poured another cup of hot coffee. He leaned down toward the electric heater at his boot and heard someone clearly saying, "*Darkness.*" The red glow from his heater faded, and the power blew inside the PERA Building.

But it hadn't. Five seconds later, power restored, Eduardo sat back on his stool, the voice hanging over him like a cliff. *Darkness.* A sharp voice. A woman's voice. Then, a swift movement passed by his janitor's room. Eduardo leaped into the hall, his flashlight bouncing over the high walls, catching sight of a woman with long black hair, clutching a black shawl to her face as if frightened. A low whimper came from behind her dark robe. Eduardo saw her fade to black as the power shut down once more.

The cold air outside the PERA Building hit Eduardo in the face as he ran out the front doors. He stopped when he reached the street and turned around, but the lights were all on again and everything looked the way it should look. At that moment, Eduardo reached into his memories for the *La Llorona* stories the *viejitos* used to tell on the Santa Fe Plaza. He always thought they were making them up.

The doors of the PERA Building swung open. Two glowing embers the size of snowballs shot out of the building and headed straight for Eduardo as he ran up the Santa Fe Trail. It was dawn when he returned to his home. His wife was just starting the fire. She wanted to know why he forgot his dinner dishes again.

Sam Welch
Beverly Hills, CA

The Man Who Wouldn't Go to Church

There was this *vato*—this guy—who never wanted to go to church. His wife was always wanting to have her husband be an example to their children, but he didn't care. He liked to sleep late on Sundays, sit around and eat doughnuts and drink coffee, read the paper, and so on. He said church services got in the way of these important activities. Besides, he told his wife, "God already knows what I believe, so who do I have to prove it to?" She left it at that. She would get the three kids up early for Sunday Mass and have them dressed and out the door by 5:30 a.m. for the walk to church. Most of the time, they'd be back before he was even out of bed.

One Saturday night during Lent, though, his wife said to him that he should at least think of her and the kids and just this once he should get dressed and go with them. Instead of being a nice guy about it, what does he do? He gets mad and goes out and gets drunk!

While he was heading home, about 3:00 or 4:00 in the morning, *La Llorona* stopped him and lectured him about his not being a good father, about how he should go to church, etc. etc. He told *La Llorona* to mind her own business! Well, that was all she needed to hear. So she took him and tied him to the door of the church, and that's where they found him the next morning. He was very mad. While his friends were untying him, he was bragging in a loud voice that *La Llorona* wasn't going to force him to do anything—he was a real stubborn guy.

But as stubborn as he was, it seems like the village residents always found this guy tied to the church doors every Sunday morning. Sometimes he'd have a black eye, or his clothes would be torn. He was always a mess. This went on for about six months, and he finally gave up. I guess he just got tired of it.

So he finally ended up making a deal with *La Llorona:* If she didn't bother the *borrachos*—the winos—in the neighborhood, and as long as they bothered no one else, he would see to it that all of the neighborhood *borrachos*, himself included, would go to church every Sunday.

So that's how a miracle occurred in that particular neighborhood.

Ruben Chavez
Santa Fe, NM

The Ride from El Ojo de La Vaca

My aunt, Ramona Martinez, used to tell me that her brother Epifanio Garcia was a very outspoken young man— this would be in 1885 or so—and very argumentative with his parents. One day, after a particularly heated argument which greatly distressed their mother, Epifanio and his two brothers, Carlos and Augustine, decided to visit the family home in the city of Santa Fe, also formally known as *La Villa Real de La Santa Fe de San Francisco de Asis*—the Royal City of the Holy Faith of Saint Francis of Assisi.

They got into their horse-drawn wagon and started the long ride from El Ojo de La Vaca, turning off on a branch of the Santa Fe Trail heading toward the old Blas Garcia land grant in the Apache Ridge area. Augustine was riding in the back of the wagon and Carlos and Epifanio were in the front, when all of a sudden there appeared on the front seat between them a very beautiful lady wearing a black *tapalo*— a shawl—with a black net over her face and big silver earrings. As they rode in the dusky light toward Santa Fe, each of the three terrified young men addressed this creature but were met with a stony silence. She stared straight ahead, never looking to her right or to her left, and acted as though she had not heard them. After a while, Epifanio moved his elbow a little to the right to see if this lady was real, and his arm seemed to go right through her. When Augustine saw this from his seat behind them, he became so terrified that he started shaking uncontrollably.

As they approached the house turning from the Santa Fe Trail onto what is now Garcia Street, she began to fade from their vision. Just before she completely vanished, she said, "I will visit you again some day when you argue with your mother." When they went into the house, they saw the light from the kerosene lamp and Augustine fainted.

Epifanio didn't change from having had this experience. He was always argumentative and ornery with people, and as a matter of fact he lived well into his 90's.

Juanita Garcia
Santa Fe, NM

The Hippie Learns a Lesson

There are many stories here in Chimayo about *La Llorona*. This is one of my favorites.

Back about 1970, the first hippies moved here. Some of them were okay, but some of them were very disrespectful. This story concerns one of the disrespectful ones, who was also a thief.

This hippie was named after some animal or bird— the hippies used names like that. He was named "Bear," or "Crow." I can't remember. Maybe it was "Mole." No, now that I think of it, "Mole" was someone else's name — a friend of his, I think. I'll call him "Bear" for the purposes of this story. He had a wife who also had a strange name like "Sunshine" or "Ocean" or something like that, and a couple of little children who ran around with runny noses and no pants or shoes. They bought a little piece of land that no one else would want and built a house that was all underground, with boards over the top for a roof. It was a terrible place to live. At least, my husband and I thought so. But who am I to judge?—"*cada chango a sun columpio* — each monkey to his own swing."

Now, this "Bear" was from California and had a very rich family, so he never had to work and he didn't have any respect for people who worked hard.

The first trouble we had with "Bear" was when he would go riding horses across our pasture and leave the gates open so the cows would get out and my poor husband would spend days chasing them back into the pasture. This caused a lot of trouble for us, believe me. A couple of people even shot in his direction, but he didn't pay any attention. He thought the land belonged to everyone and there shouldn't be any fences, but my husband says, "Good fences make good neighbors."

The other thing we all thought was strange was that this hippie had some idea he was an Indian. We would see him riding his horse along the arroyo and all he wore was this little leather thing like Tarzan, with beads and feathers around his neck and moccasins.

People tried to ignore this "Bear," but soon they started to notice signs that something had been in their gardens. At first it was like the skunks do when they get at the corn, with all the ears broken off. Then, other vegetables started to disappear and some fruit, too. We soon realized it wasn't a skunk—not the four-legged kind, anyway.

Nobody had caught "Bear" stealing, but people knew it was him anyway. As we say up here in the north, "*Cuando el sarten chilla, algo hay en la villa*—When the frying pan sizzles, something's up in the village."

So, this stealing went on through the summer and then, that fall—in October, I think—it all stopped. We had a long summer that year with no frost in September, so there was still food in many gardens. One of the best gardens belonged to Mrs. Martinez and she told me this story.

Late one night in this particular October, when the moon was almost full and the leaves were dry and rustling on the trees, Mrs. Martinez could not sleep. She has sciatica, *pobrecita,* so she was up at her table late, drinking *atole* and looking out the window. Hearing a noise, she looked closer and saw this "Bear" in her garden with a sack and all of a sudden she realized that he was taking her carrots! He was wearing his Tarzan costume and had smeared himself with something dark like mud, probably so he couldn't be seen.

The wind was blowing that night, so there were noises from the loose tin on Mrs. Martinez' roof and the tree branches. Now, you should know that Mrs. Martinez' garden is right below the Martinez *acequia*, which is the big one that runs through the plaza, and it is well known that *La Llorona* likes the ditches.

So, as Mrs. Martinez was watching this "Bear" through her window, she heard the wind really start to howl louder and louder. Then she realized that it was not just the wind—it was the cry of *La Llorona!* She saw this "Bear" straighten up all of a sudden after bending over the carrot patch, and even through the mud on his face, she could see his eyes get big. Across the ditch came floating *La Llorona,* tall like she is, and all dressed in black, increasing her howling by the minute. The "Bear" dropped poor Mrs. Martinez' carrots and began to run. He was so scared he ran right into the fence and fell down. He tried to get up, but his body failed him and so he scrambled along on all fours.

All along the road, as "Bear" ran, the howling continued and all the porch lights came on and the dogs began to bark. Everyone saw "Bear," running as fast as he could, his Indian braids standing out straight behind him as he ran for his life.

After that night, this "Bear" took his family to live somewhere else. He is probably still stealing because, as we all know, "*La zorra mudara los dientes pero no las mientes*—The fox may lose its teeth but not its ways."

But, thanks to *La Llorona,* this doesn't happen in our village anymore.

Refugio Archuleta
Chimayo, NM

The Mystery of Ramona Sena

My uncle told me that this incident happened up in the *milpas*, the gardening areas of Cerro Gordo in Santa Fe, in the early 1700's. This is a true story that has been passed on down through the generations in my own family.

A woman had been working in the gardens, picking corn and squash, and she had set her baby down under a tree while she worked. It was her first day on the job and she was new to the area, having come down from Tierra Amarilla a few days before. It was late summer and very beautiful. The crops were especially plentiful that particular year, and many farmers were using extra workers from wherever they could find them.

Later in the day, the *patron*—the owner—sent a message from his house that he wanted to see her, so she asked one of the other women, also a new worker by the name of Ramona Sena, to watch the baby while she walked the mile or so to this owner's house on Cerro Gordo. She walked quickly, and arrived only moments before a violent rainstorm came on.

A while later, all of the workers appeared in front of the house because it did not appear that the rain would stop and they could no longer work in the downpour. The young mother looked out the window at the little group of people, and then suddenly ran to the door, asking, "Where is Ramona Sena who was caring for my baby?" The people looked at each other and then said, "Ramona? No one has seen her for the past year or so." The young mother broke away from the group and ran in the pouring rain back to the *milpas*. She could not find Ramona or her baby.

La Llorona Original
TN87012601
Tony Sandoval

To this day, they say it was *La Llorona* who had taken on the form of Ramona Sena. No one has seen Ramona Sena since, and the baby was never found.

Many of the old-timers say that *La Llorona* takes on different forms of women to confuse and frighten people, while at other times she does it to help people.

John R. Sandoval
Santa Fe, NM

The Woman in White

I am 84 years old and live in El Llano de San Juan, a mountain village situated off the high road to Taos, east of Penasco. It is very beautiful up here. In the old days, El Llano de San Juan was (and still is) a stronghold of the *Penitentes*, which is an offshoot of the early teachings of Catholicism. Some people say that after the Spaniards deserted the mountain villages in New Mexico, these people were left without religious leaders and so developed the *Penitente* beliefs and practices. Others say they originated in Spain and were brought to this country by the Spanish *conquistadores*. Whatever the case may be, these *Penitentes* are humble people and their home is your home—*mi casa es su casa*. You are treated like royalty when you visit them.

I play the violin at *Rancho de Las Golindrinas* in Santa Fe— the Ranch of the Swallows—an indoor-outdoor museum that recreates the style of living here as it was in the early days when this part of the country was known as *Nueva Espana*—New Spain—with weavers, religious observations, people cooking native dishes, and so on. There is a festival in October of each year that attracts thousands of people.

I used to live in El Turquillo, an area between Mora and Guadalupita. "El Turquillo" means "The Turk." We are not sure how it got that name, but perhaps it is because the Spanish settlers of that area were descendants of the Turkish clans that ruled Spain during the days of the Moors.

In 1930 or 1931, we were sitting by our house in El Turquillo. It was a special occasion, and we had some of our sons, there too. We had many cows. It was in the afternoon, and we were sitting by the house looking down the Lucero road. There is a little creek there that comes in from Guadalupita. We were gossiping and talking when all of a sudden, we saw a woman from the direction

of Guadalupita. She was dressed in white. A very tall woman, at least nine feet tall. The whole family gathered in the yard to watch her. It gave me the chills.

She came down to the bottom of the ravine and started walking on the Lucero road, which is in front of our house, and then when she got to the spot where she had to cross the river, she just seemed to float over the water. Then she started going up the hill and when she got to the top, she disappeared in thin air. At a distance of about 500 yards, she reappeared. We watched her until she disappeared a second time.

Another time, we saw her doing the same thing. We could not tell if she wore shoes—she might have been barefooted. Her dress was very long. We checked but found no tracks. People said then that she was *La Llorona*.

Patricio Lujan
Rodarte, NM

The Best Horseman of All

Many years ago on a ranch in Trujillo, New Mexico, near Las Vegas, there lived a boy about 15 years old who loved to ride horses more than anything. He had a pony and dreamed of having a horse when he was older, but his father had told him that he would first have to become a good horseman, even an excellent one, before he could have a horse of his own. One afternoon, when he was discussing this with one of the ranch hands, the ranch hand said to him, "There is one way that you can become the finest horseman for miles around. You know that cave about three miles from here? *La Llorona* lives there. You have to go see her and offer your soul to her." The ranch hand also told the boy that *La Llorona* was only awake after dark, as she slept all day like a vampire. This meant, he said, that the boy would have to leave the ranch in the late afternoon so that he would still be able to find his way to the cave, but he would have to time it in such a way that he would arrive when it was dark. He also explained that La Llorona was a *bruja*— a witch—so would know if he was coming or not, and that she would be at the cave's entrance to greet him.

The boy had never been to that cave, but he had passed by it on his pony many times. It was a very deep, dark cave, well hidden from the regular path that people used, and the entrance was at the bottom of a steep, rocky hill lined with strange, dead little trees with branches that reached out and scratched you until you bled. Quite frankly, he was a little nervous at the idea of going into this cave, and even more nervous that he would see *La Llorona* face to face. However, at the age of 15 he was inexperienced and quite foolish, and so the idea of sacrificing his soul did not really bother him very much—not if it meant having a horse at last!

So that afternoon at about four o'clock, he took his pony and started out toward the cave. He rode for about two hours, being careful not to go too fast or too slow so that he would arrive at the cave just after dusk. The sun began to descend in the west, finally, and soon the sky had turned a beautiful scarlet. Bravely, he rode on. Minutes later, it was dusk and the cave was only a little ways down the path. In a minute or two, he would meet the famous *La Llorona* face to face. And all he would have to do was give his soul to her.

He began to wonder what that would mean, exactly. Would he have to lie down in a coffin? Would he have to sign a contract of some kind? Or did he just hand his soul over to her? And, if so, how would he know how to do that? He realized that, being experienced in doing this sort of thing, she would probably tell him what he had to do and that would be that. Then he would just go home, right? He became confused. He really didn't understand what a soul was, but he had seen a book once on the subject, and it seemed as though you belonged to the person who bought your soul from you, and it was impossible to get it back, if he remembered correctly. He tried to imagine what it would be like belonging to *La Llorona*. Maybe he would have to give up his mother and father and move into the cave with her! And sleep hanging by his feet, like a bat! He shuddered at the thought. It was almost dark, now. The air had cooled considerably but he could feel little beads of sweat where he had been trying to grow a mustache.

He stopped his pony at the top of the path and looked down toward the cave's entrance. He could barely see it in the dim light. It seemed as though the branches on the little dead trees were moving slightly. He thought he heard something rustling nearby. Perhaps *La Llorona* sensed his presence and was coming to the entrance to greet him. As he sat there on his pony and contemplated his future in the hands of *La Llorona,* as the last light of the sun disappeared behind the distance mountains, he decided to go home and think about this a little more—perhaps a lot more.

He turned the pony around and headed home. When he got there, his dog excitedly ran to him and jumped at him in the dark, knocking him down. Well, that was all it took. He passed out cold. When he came to, he found himself on the couch in front of the wood stove. His mother had made him some hot *atole* and there was a little plate of apple-filled *empanaditas*. He was awfully glad to see her and his dad. He sat by the fire and thought about how much he appreciated them and loved them.

He soon became an excellent horseman. By the time he was 17, he had won numerous blue ribbons and awards. And he was very, very glad that he had finally decided to go back and visit *La Llorona* after that first night of doubt.

Cosme Garcia
Santa Fe, NM

Sister Cleo's Revelation

The Loretto Academy, a girls school, used to be situated where the Inn at Loretto is now. Across the street was where Fred West, the very popular and well-respected Justice of the Peace, had his office. This street was, of course, the original Santa Fe Trail that went to La Fonda Hotel.

Sister Cleofitas was an old and beautiful nun who was perhaps no more than four and a half feet tall, and who would often walk up the Old Santa Fe Trail to the old *camposanto*—cemetery—across from the Boyle greenhouse, where they specialized in carnations of all colors. Sister Cleofitas visited the *camposanto* often to place carnations on some of the graves and to keep the headstones clean. Each year, when the fruit blossoms appeared on the trees, she would spend many hours cleaning and weeding the areas around the graves with her rake and hoe. She was a kind, thoughtful, and generous person who truly loved God and her calling as a sister in her order, but the older she grew, the more she began to miss some of the nuns who had passed away before her, and who were now being replaced by young novices. Sometimes, she would stand at the graves and talk to Sister Rosina and Sister Angelica, who lay side by side, and she would cry quietly into her little hands when she thought of the seemingly lonely years that lay ahead.

Late one hot summer afternoon, Sister Cleo was pulling some particularly stubborn weeds from around the headstone of Sister Miguela, and she was having a great deal of trouble pulling one weed that was nearly as tall as she was. As she struggled and puffed, she began to sense that she was not alone, and looked up to see a very tall woman in black standing over her. For a moment, Sister Cleo thought that the woman was another sister, but then realized that she was a stranger and wore a shawl over her head and had a pale and sad face. Sister Cleo squinted up at the lady, who asked her what she was doing. Sister Cleo, surprised, answered: "I am here to make certain that the flowers at the graves of the sisters are fresh and watered. It is only right to do so in honor of the dead."

The sad-faced woman said to Sister Cleo, "I cannot bury my children, for I cannot find them. They are lost in time and space, and it is my fate to search for them until the end of eternity. You have your friends right here, safe and protected. But they cannot smell the scent of these flowers —take them to someone who can smell them." With these words, the woman faded away. Sister Cleo was naturally very startled by this encounter and shaken to her tiny little feet by these words of wisdom imparted to her.

Sister Cleo turned and began to walk toward the setting sun, leaving the hoe and the rake behind and the weeds in an untidy little pile. She walked past the unseeing eyes of Sister Angelica and Sister Rosina and Sister Miguela. She continued past the front gate and down the dirt road towards the greenhouses. From there, she walked west towards the Loretto Academy. She continued past the Loretto Academy, moving more and more swiftly until her tiny little feet became a blur and she herself seemed to be carried by an unearthly wind.

It is said that Sister Cleofitas next appeared in India, ministering to the beggers and lepers. Many said that they had seen her that afternoon passing the Academy, and that she was young again and very beautiful like an angel.

Orlinda Tapia
San Antonio, TX

 # The Rabbit Coat

In Villanueva, New Mexico, in the area south of the river by the old arroyo, was a place where the villagers used to dump their trash. While it was a well-known fact that *La Llorona* haunted arroyos, she was also frequently seen in various dump areas. The people used to say that they would see her at this particular dump area on Saturdays—never any other day.

In 1918, when I was still a little girl, my grandmother, Maria Isabel, told me that my grandfather, Juan Del Rio, took his .22 rifle out one morning to hunt for rabbit, and when he returned the next day, he told her that he had shared fried rabbit with a very strange woman dressed in black who kept whimpering and looking around as though she had lost something. He had never seen this lady in any of the surrounding villages or ranches — and he knew everyone for miles around.

It seems that he had gone out to the dump area on this particular Saturday, and had shot a rabbit near the arroyo. This was a good place, of course, for finding rabbit because they would look for food there. He was roasting it and cleaning the *cuero*—the skin—when this lady appeared out of nowhere and asked if he would share the rabbit with her because she was very hungry and tired from looking for her little boy and little girl. My grandpa was a very kind-hearted person, very generous, and very sociable. He gave her his *zalea* —sheepskin—that he kept rolled up on his horse for warmth because she was *temblando*—shivering—and he told her to make herself comfortable by the fire.

While they were eating the rabbit, she very sadly told my grandpa that her children had wandered off to play when their wagon train had stopped to water the horses. Knowing that no wagon train had come through that area for many years, my grandpa asked her exactly when this had happened, and she replied, "Oh, about the time we first came here from the south, maybe 100 or 150 years ago." Then she told him she was going to her cave and would return with a gift for his wife, and she disappeared. He got up and looked around trying to see what had happened to the *cuero del conejo,* the rabbitskin, and realized that she had taken it with her but had left the *zalea* behind.

Grandma Isabel said that a week later they got up to go to church and found a beautiful rabbit skin coat by the front door with a note written in very beautiful and educated script that said, "Juan Del Rio, you are a good man to strangers and this gift for your wife is from a lady that wanders the earth looking for the good in man and her lost children."

My grandmother wore that coat for many, many years and it never showed any signs of wear.

Maclovia Guerin
Denver, CO

La Llorona de La Junta

I was born in Missouri and lived for a time in La Junta, Colorado, a small town of about 8,000 people, and there were nine kids in my family, four older than me, and four younger. La Junta is basically desert, but the land is used for raising cattle.

We were a close-knit family—a clan, really—and I took care of my two younger sisters, but I hung around with my two younger brothers every chance I got. I was a tomboy and we pretty much ran wild. We used to take long hikes in the summer through fields full of rattlesnake— sometimes you'd see 20 or 30 of them either basking in the sun or lying asleep under rocks. Occasionally, I could hear them rattle but I was never afraid. We'd learned somewhere that if you were quiet and respectful, they'd never bother you. We also used to see lots of scorpions and tarantulas. It wasn't unusual for the temperature to get up to 120. One time, we fried some eggs on the sidewalk near our house and our mother caught us. She was very angry because eggs were a precious commodity for a family of nine kids.

In the 1960's, I was attending a Catholic school, and I guess I was about 13 or 14 when a bunch of us decided one summer night that it might be fun to go to the cemetery with candles and a ouija board and call up some spirits. In retrospect, I can't believe that we used to do that, because I personally think it's very dangerous. But we visited the cemetery every chance we got that summer.

We actually used to hear voices around the graves. My friends would say to me, "That's *La Llorona* coming to get you, Barbara, because you're blonde, and *La Llorona's* lost child is blonde, too. So if she comes here, she'll grab you and not any of us." I bought this ridiculous story and was really frightened by it, but for some reason I never ran out of there and went home.

When we weren't using the ouija board, we used to talk about *La Llorona*. She was an endlessly fascinating subject for us. We continued to do this calling up of the spirits for another summer before we decided that there were more interesting things to do, like go out with boys, for example.

Now and then we'd also go down to this area where there was an arroyo with a wooden bridge running across it. It ran in July of every year, and we'd stand around on the bridge and throw rocks into the water and talk about how *La Llorona* was looking for her two kids that had died somehow—I don't recall if any of us really knew how they had died—but the story was that if she found us she'd take our spirits. This particular bridge held a special attraction for us because we used to hear a terrible, eerie, plaintive wailing that seemed to travel from underneath the bridge and up the sides of the arroyo. I can't describe to you how very much it actually sounded like a woman wailing. It was the wind, of course, and I'm sure a meteorologist or physicist could explain the dynamics of that to me now, but at the time we much preferred to believe that it was *La Llorona* we were hearing.

Strangely enough, I now live in an area of Santa Fe on the Acequia Madre where there have been many, many sightings of *La Llorona* over the years. Sometimes, when I am out walking my dog, I imagine that I can hear her wailing nearby. I am a weaver by profession and now I'm trying to incorporate my idea of her into some of my landscape tapestries. Now that I think of it, it seems amazing that *La Llorona* has been a part of my life in one way or another since I was in elementary school.

Barbara Berger
Santa Fe, NM

# The Robe

As a young boy growing up in the Belen area in the early 1950's, there were many times when I used to hear the story of *La Llorona*. There were several versions, but the one I used to hear the most often from my grandmother was that *La Llorona* had lost her two children and desperately needed to find them, and that she might see a child who looked like one of hers, and she would start screaming in agony. The reason she was always near the river was because that's where she had lost them, supposedly by drowning. My grandma also used to say that *La Llorona* had the ability to judge others because she lived in another world where the past, present, and future were one.

My understanding of *La Llorona* came into play during the summer of 1956, when Billy Segura moved into the neighborhood. Billy and I were both 12 years old and we hit it off right away. I liked Billy because he was afraid of absolutely nothing. He brazenly smoked Pall Malls, cussed up a storm, and dismissed as "stupid" all of the things that I had been taught to value from birth. Not only that, he talked about getting himself tattooed when he was 16 and joining the Navy. Billy was from Los Angeles and knew everything—a real sophisticated kind of a guy, I thought. My parents differed on this appraisal and forbade me to associate with him in any way whatsoever.

I was an obedient, well-behaved kid and I tried to oblige my parents but it was pretty useless in the face of Billy's constant insistence that we break the rules whenever possible. He also berated me for being "chicken" and for allowing my parents and grandmother to "push me around." This was around the time of the Korean conflict and there was a lot of publicity in the papers about American soldiers being brainwashed by the Koreans. Billy warned me about losing my ability to even reason in the face of their manipulation. I was putty in his hands.

I began climbing out of my bedroom window some nights to meet Billy and his wayward friends down by the river, or at the dump, or wherever they decided to congregate. Most of his friends were older kids—some of them even had their own cars and they carried chains or tire irons around the way some women carry purses. They had nicknames like "Killer" or "Loco" or "Hitter," and I found out that one of the major reasons they all met so late at night was for the purpose of acquiring parts to their automobiles at minimal, if any, cost.

I began to wise up at some point and realized I was in over my head. I knew it was a matter of time before I would be placed on assignment as a "runner" or something illegal. I was also growing tired of this deception and I was still young and impressionable enough to fear my grandmother, fear *La Llorona,* fear my parents, and fear punishment. One hot night in August, I snuck home with a new resolve—I would not see Billy Segura or his weird friends anymore. I carefully removed the screen, climbed into my bedroom in the usual way, replaced the screen, and got into bed.

As I lay back against the cool pillow, relieved that I had finally made this decision to straighten out my twisted and corrupt life, I happened to look down toward the end of my bed, and there she was, the light of the half moon showcasing her like a Renaissance painting in a museum—*La Llorona,* seated in my rocking chair, as motionless as a statue. As I lay there in a state of complete terror, my eyes riveted to her darkened but distinctive form, a cloud moved across the moon and plunged us both into near total darkness. As the minutes—and then hours—ticked by on my trusty little alarm clock, *La Llorona* continued her vigil, staring at me in final judgment of my deeds. I knew, then, that it was probably too late to do anything—it was your classic example of the sinner repenting, only to find out that Judgment Day had already arrived, that the Grim Reaper—or, in this case, *La Llorona*—was already at the door.

I could see that she looked almost exactly as I had always pictured her, with the exception of a long braid that fell over her left shoulder. And, despite the heat of that endless summer night, she wore her dark cloak securely wrapped around her with a hood that almost completely covered her pale, twisted, and ancient face. Her mouth lay slackly open as if prepared to emit a silent scream, and I could see tiny little fangs glistening in the dim moonlight. As I lay there waiting for death or whatever fate *La Llorona* had chosen for me, I thought of my loving family, of this wonderful house we lived in, of the beans and chile and tortillas that I would never taste again in the awful netherworld that I would call home for all eternity. And I wondered why *La Llorona* was not sitting in Billy Segura's bedroom instead of mine. What had I ever done to deserve this?

And so, I have come to the end of my story. As you can see, I am still here. Of course, it was not *La Llorona* sitting in my rocking chair that August night. It was my bathrobe, a dark brown corduroy thing thrown carelessly over the back of the chair, a robe that my mother had made on her Singer sewing machine. It was an unusual bathrobe because it had a gold braid that served as a tie around the waist, which used to be a pull for some old draperies we had in the basement. And it had a hood that I could wear over my head on those cold nights when it was necessary to make a trip to the outhouse.

To this day, I regard the dawn as the most exciting, revealing part of the day, when a person is most susceptible to learning the truth about life.

What happened to Billy Segura? I have no idea. His family moved back to Los Angeles a few months later. I am glad I knew him for that brief period, though—the best lessons are always learned early in life.

Robert Gonzales
Rio Rancho, NM

Uncle Manuel and La Llorona

During the early 1930's, the United States Government employed the youth of the Santa Fe area in constructing forest access roads, dams for soil conservation, and riprapping rock around the Santa Fe River. At that time, the teenagers and younger kids had more respect for adults, and the so-called civil rights of the young were controlled by the adults. The judicial system did not discolor the facts of life as it does now. In fact, *La Llorona* was the instrument used by the grandpas to keep order, and believe me, it worked extremely well.

Uncle Manuel was a teenager in those days, and his job was to chop the wood, gather kindling, bring in water from the outside hand-dug well, empty out the ashes from the wood-burning stoves, and keep the kerosene lamps full.

Our family on Garcia Street, having owned homes there since before it was named Garcia Street, tells us that my dad, Carlos Garcia, said *La Llorona* came from the direction of Camino Las Animas between the Andy Rivera and Jesus Baca driveway, and that she stood on the Garcia Street side and cried in a very low whimper. If you read the book, "The Squaw Tree," by Alice Bullock, it even says in there that *La Llorona* used to wail and cry in that area.

Uncle Manuel would not go out after dark for firewood or do his chores. Once the sun set, he would hide behind the stove. This was the same man who later was highly decorated while fighting under General Mark Clark in Africa, having received the Bronze Star for the African Campaign, the Sicilian Campaign, and the Italian Campaign, and all kinds of battle stars. He was the hero of our family.

You ask him now, and he will tell you how as a youngster he was kept in line by the legendary *La Llorona*.

Juanita Garcia
Santa Fe, NM

The Last Dance

On Labor Day in 1952, the last day of *Fiestas* in Santa Fe, one of my sisters passed away. I was 12 years old and part of a large family. While the members of my family grieved her loss, the rest of the city celebrated the most important and exciting weekend of the entire year. My father sent the younger children, including myself, out of the house and told us to keep busy doing other things while they made funeral arrangements and received visitors. My dad had one strict rule, though: be home by midnight.

So I spent the day and evening wandering around and observing the various events. Everyone was dressed up in their *Fiesta* outfits—the ladies in full ruffled skirts and fancy blouses, wearing all their finest turquoise and silver, and the men in Mexican *charro* outfits or their best Spanish *torero*—bullfighter— costumes. There were *villeros alegres* who played their guitars or fiddles, while others danced in the streets or went to private parties. This was, and still is, a weekend when everyone, and I mean everyone, celebrates.

As the day—and then evening—wore on, I found myself in the area of the old Guadalupe Bridge, which was near the Five Points Liquor Store property and where *El Baile*—the final dance of the *Fiesta* weekend—was taking place. Hundreds of people swirled around in the lot next to the store in colorful costumes to music from *mariachis*. The atmosphere was electric with excitement and many dancers spilled out into the streets and mingled with people who were passing by and had stopped to watch. I found myself watching from the sidelines with several others who were too young or too shy to participate. While I was not really involved because of the sadness I was feeling at the time, I was still mesmerized by the magic of that evening.

There were other people besides myself who were passive participants, one of them an elderly woman of about 80. I noticed her several times that evening, probably because no matter where I wandered, she always seemed to be a few feet away. It didn't seem unusual, though, since there were also several other people I kept seeing here and there.

At some point, I suddenly realized that it was almost midnight and that no matter how fast I ran home, I would never make it on time. But I decided to try anyway, and so I started doing a fast jog across the bridge and toward our house, which was a half a mile away on West Manhattan Street. As I trotted along, I began to realize that someone was behind me and keeping up with me no matter how fast I ran. When I hit the corner on Romero Street, I glanced back to see who it was and almost fell over when I realized it was the same little old lady I had seen back at *El Baile*. At that point I really put some smoke behind me and practically fell when I stumbled to our back door, which was unfortunately locked. I banged and banged with my fists, but everyone was in front of the house and couldn't hear me, I guess. I was too scared to turn around and see if the old lady was approaching, but I imagined that she was practically on top of me. Finally, I ran around the front and threw myself, completely out of breath, at the feet of my surprised family. I was never so glad to see a group of people in my life as I was at that moment. When I told my dad what had happened, he said to me, "It's all in your mind—it's because of your sister." But he went outside and looked around anyway, just to make sure.

There were a lot of *La Llorona* stories floating around in those days, just as there always have been. Many of the stories revolved around the idea that if a person misbehaved, they'd run into *La Llorona*. But in this case, I'd done nothing wrong, and so I wonder to this day about that incident, even though no one can ever convince me it wasn't *La Llorona* herself chasing me down that street.

Sometimes people would say to someone who had seen *La Llorona*, "You've had too much *mula*," which was the home-made whiskey the local people made out of corn or potatoes. I hardly need to tell you that the strongest thing I drank on that terrible night, at the tender age of 12, was a Coke.

My dad used to make beer in our bathtub—no one could use the tub for the three or four days it would take to ferment. Then he'd put it in bottles he'd collected—you never threw away bottles in those days because someone could always use them. Once in a while one of them would explode and it sounded like a gun going off. I remember seeing a kitchen cabinet door hanging by one hinge because a bottle on the shelf had blown up. God was looking out for us in those days because none of us ever got hit by flying glass.

You might ask why we didn't use kegs, which we could get at Theo Roybal's store. He sold the glass ones—I think they came from Mexico—but they were too small, really. Before that, folks used to use metal kegs and they'd poison the heck out of themselves because the beer interacted with the metal somehow and made people really sick.

Folks used to say, "On that stuff, you'd see anything." I guess that's true with the *borrachos*, anyway—all of them talk about *La Llorona!*

Herman Grace
Santa Fe, NM

 *The Tiny Screamer*

There was a real short guy, no more than maybe five feet or five feet one, by the name of Padilla. He was the *mayordomo* of the Acequia Madre in Santa Fe, the "mother ditch" that flows into the Santa Fe River. The *mayordomo* is the person who is assigned to supervise the maintenance of the *acequias* by the residents of a given neighborhood or *barrio*. In the older days, this assignment assured that everyone would have irrigation water for their gardens, that it flowed nicely, and there was no debris in it. The *mayordomo* is still a very prestigious and important position in all of the villages of northern New Mexico, and it is a great honor to be given the title. I understand that the Federal government has put aside millions of dollars for these villages to use to work on their *acequias*, as a matter of fact.

Anyway, to get back to the story, this guy Padilla was always down at the Acequia Madre. He took his job very seriously. He spent all of his time clearing the weeds and rocks that the kids used to throw in there. In those days—now, this would be in the 1920's—you didn't have beer cans, soda cans, candy wrappers, all this junk that people throw on the ground now. People used to save any liquor bottles or other bottles they had. They always could find another use for them. In fact, no one threw anything away in those days.

One evening, Padilla was around San Antonio Street and Acequia Madre, right around where the elementary school is now. This was in the late spring and there were weeds everywhere, and he had been pulling them for quite some time and had made a little pile of them in the road that he planned to burn later. Something made him look up, and there was this little tiny boy standing across the road, and the kid was crying up a storm, weeping and wailing and just creating a real racket. Now, Padilla was a nice guy and he had kids of his own, and his heart just about melted seeing this tiny little kid in some kind of trouble, so he started across the road to get a better look at the boy and to see who he belonged to. As he started toward him, though, the kid started screaming even louder. And the louder he screamed, the taller he seemed to grow. So by the time Padilla got to him, the kid was as tall as Padilla and still growing, and his screaming was deafening. Padilla dropped his rake and ran like hell with his hands over his ears. He turned around at one point, just to take a peek while he was running, and you're going to say I'm lying, but the kid was probably a good nine feet tall and still growing.

From that day forward, Padilla told everyone that he had seen *La Llorona's* son. He said the way the kid grew so fast was a perfect example of an old Spanish saying: "*Tanto hace el diablo con su hijo hasta que lo mata*—The devil does so much with his son until he kills him"—and that is the way the story is told to this day by the old timers in that neighborhood.

Alfonso "Trompo" Trujillo
Santa Fe, NM

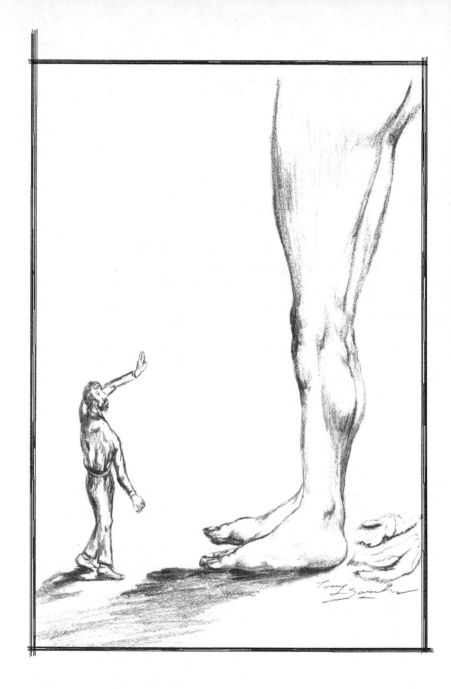

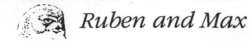

Ruben and Max

In May of 1940, Ruben and Max were employed as grave diggers at the San Jose Cemetery on Rincon Street in Las Vegas. This was a Catholic cemetery which also had the reputation of being *La Llorona's* hunting grounds. There had been many sightings of her in this area over the years, and few men wanted to take the job of grave digger despite the fact that there was hardly any work to go around in those days.

Now, this was during World War II and people were nervous anyway because nearly everyone had a relative fighting overseas, or knew someone who had been killed or wounded. It was not a time for *La Llorona* to be scaring people—there was already enough on their minds. But, since folks had the jitters from always thinking about death, now they talked about *La Llorona* more than ever. There were stories about her all over Las Vegas, and it seemed like a good many of these stories started on Saturday nights in the *cantinas* and then spread to the *barrios* from there.

Max and Ruben were digging a grave around this time in preparation of the burial of a Mr. Armijo, who would have been 94 years old had he been able to stay on this earth for just another week. As the saying goes, however, "*pero ya quando Dios se acuerda de ti*—But when God remembers you, you're gone."

It was Good Friday, as a matter of fact, and the hour was growing late as the two men labored over the last *paladas de tierra*—shovels of dirt. They stopped for a few minutes to partake of some vintage wine that they had purchased a little earlier on their way to work. Ruben sniffed the cork to make sure it was the wine he was accustomed to drinking, and nodded in satisfaction—*gracias a Dios* that *vino de pata* still could be had for a decent price from the bootleggers. It was and always would be his favorite beverage.

As the two men rested against a cottonwood tree and shared the bottle of *vino de pata*, they looked up at the full moon as it began its ascent on the darkening horizon. At that moment, however, their peace was shattered by a terrible loud cry and the two startled men suddenly saw themselves looking straight at the figure of a woman in white striding toward them in the dusk. Max and Ruben, although they had never seen her before, instinctively knew that this was *La Llorona*. She quickened her approach toward them, her arms outstretched as if to grab them. At the same time, she let out a terrible, low wail that sounded like a wounded animal. Ruben and Max jumped to their feet and ran from the cemetery, never to return again.

Now, every time Ruben and Max get drunk—which unfortunately is often—they talk about this experience with *La Llorona*. They have told this same story in every *cantina*. It is always the same but for one little detail: they say it happened on Bad Friday, not Good Friday.

Raymond Lovato
Las Vegas, NM

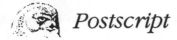 *Postscript*

On the night I finished proofreading the manuscript for this book, I had a very bizarre experience which I am sure is connected to *La Llorona*. Two days later, another strange thing occurred, and I believe very strongly that these events are interconnected. Both occurred at my house near Rodeo Road in Santa Fe, which I understand to be an area that had many *La Llorona* sightings before the developers came in in the 1960's. Before then, Rodeo Road and its surroundings was a desolate but beautiful area full of arroyos where people came to hunt rabbits, ride horses, etc.

The first incident occurred one night in February, 1988, when I was telling my husband about some of the stories I had read that day—in particular, I was recalling the one by Tony Sanchez, the illustrator, where *La Llorona* appears to him in a dream and says, "You shouldn't draw me if you don't believe in me." My husband was lying in bed and I was standing outside the doorway of the bedroom as I related Tony's experience. I had just turned my back and was walking away, when I felt a presence behind me, just inside the bedroom door. The presence was so intense and so real to me that I turned around to see who was there. Of course, there was no one, but I felt as though I could have reached out and easily touched whoever it was.

Two days later, I was alone in the house with my two young sons, then four and six. We were all seated at the kitchen table, eating supper. Suddenly, Robert, the little one, turned and looked in the direction of the same place where I had felt the presence two days before. He jumped down from the chair and yelled "Daddy!" and ran toward something that only he could see, his arms outstretched in anticipation. Frightened, I also jumped up and ran after Robert and grabbed his shoulders. "What did you see?" I asked him.

For the next few minutes, Robert insisted that he had seen someone. Finally, he said, "Maybe it was a cat." When he understood that it could not have been a cat, either, he said to me, "I saw something there, and it was gray." He would not back down from this story. What he saw was as real to him as anything he had ever seen.

I sat the boys down at the table again and forced myself to walk through the house. I checked the closets, under the beds, everywhere. The windows and doors were locked. We were alone in the house.

Someone told me later that *La Llorona* will sometimes appear to women with young children. Remembering that my neighbor also has two little boys, I mentioned it to her the next day and asked her if she had ever had a similar experience or if she had ever heard a woman weeping in the greenbelt area next to her house. She looked at me strangely and said, "How funny you should ask me that. Last weekend, I heard a terrible scream. At first, I thought it might be a cat, but it didn't sound like a cat."

I believe that what my neighbor heard, and what my son saw, was *La Llorona*, returning to convince me (and anyone else), as she had Tony Sanchez, that she was real. So, here is a word to the wise: Do not read these stories with a skeptical heart, or you, too, may summon *La Llorona* to your home!

Lisa Sena
Santa Fe, NM

Do You Have a Story?

The publishers are always looking for new and unusual stories, particularly those having to do with Spanish culture. They do not have to be *La Llorona* stories, although those are certainly our favorites! In fact, we would like to see any story that you think is interesting, especially if it involves an experience you or someone you know has had with the supernatural—*el sobrenatural o algunas mentiras*. If you think you have one that we can use, please send it to us. For your efforts, we will send you a *La Llorona* button.

Please fill out and return the release of information form on the next page. Don't be afraid that your story isn't good enough. Lots of the people who donated the stories in this book thought the same thing.

Please send your story to:

La Casa de La Llorona
P.O. Box 5699
Santa Fe, NM 87502-5699

Story Release Form

I, _____, residing at
　(Please Print)

_____
(Street or P.O. Box)　　　　　(City)　　　　　(State/Zip Code)

on _____, 19___, donate,
give, and contribute the following story, entitled:

_____
(Please give your story a name)

to The Word Process to be used at their discretion in their books, plays, scripts, or other creations, for the purpose stated in Certificate File #TN87012601, Office of the Secretary of the State of New Mexico.

"La Llorona Stories" become the sole property of The Word Process, and credit for same on any publications by The Word Process is sole compensation to me for this contribution noted above.

Signed:

_____

(_____) _____
(Telephone Number)

Book Order Form

To: The Word Process
P.O. Box 5699
Santa Fe, New Mexico 87502-5699

Please send me ___ copies of your book entitled:
The Weeping Woman: Encounters with La Llorona
at the incredibly low price of $9.95 each (shipping and handling
paid by The Word Process). I understand that I may return any
book for a full refund if I am not satisfied.

Name _____

Address _____

City _____ State ____ Zip _____

New Mexico residents: Please add applicable sales tax.
If this is a library book, please photocopy this page.

- - - ✂ -

Book Order Form

To: The Word Process
P.O. Box 5699
Santa Fe, New Mexico 87502-5699

Please send me ___ copies of your book entitled:
The Weeping Woman: Encounters with La Llorona
at the incredibly low price of $9.95 each (shipping and handling
paid by The Word Process). I understand that I may return any
book for a full refund if I am not satisfied.

Name _____

Address _____

City _____ State ____ Zip _____

New Mexico residents: Please add applicable sales tax.
If this is a library book, please photocopy this page.

La Llorona T-Shirt Order Form

The Word Process is offering its popular *La Llorona* T-shirts in an *American-made* 50% poly/50% cotton (non-shrink) blend with the name and copyrighted image of *La Llorona* as designed by the late Joe D'Igalo, former Walt Disney colleague. To order one or more of these beautiful T-shirts at this **special postpaid price**, please fill out the order form below and send check or money order to (please allow 3-4 weeks for delivery):

The Word Process
P.O. Box 5699
Santa Fe, New Mexico 87502-5699

Name_____

Address_____

City_____ State_____ Zip:_____

A) Gold with black ink design $10.00
B) Turquoise with silver design $15.00
C) Turquoise with gold design $15.00
D) Black with silver design $15.00
E) Black with gold design $15.00

Sizes: **XL** (46-48), **L** (42-44), **M** (38-40), and **S** (32-34)

HOW MANY	COLOR (SEE LIST ABOVE)	SIZE	PRICE EACH	TOTAL
		TOTAL ENCLOSED		

Special Discount Rates for Quantity Orders:2-5 shirts = 10% discount; 6-10 shirts =15% discount; 11 or more = 20% discount

DEALER INQUIRIES WELCOME

Edward Garcia Kraul was born in Santa Fe and grew up in East Los Angeles. He returned to Santa Fe as a young adult after serving in the Ninth Air Force. He comes from the Garcias on Garcia Street, as well as the Romero and Rodriguez families. His father was from Denmark. He is married to Judith Beatty.

Judith Beatty owns and operates The Word Process with her husband. She also takes minutes for various committees and commissions, including the Santa Fe City Council. She comes from a family of writers.

Tony Sanchez is a peer counselor for the New Vistas Independent Living Center in Santa Fe, is working toward a liberal arts degree, and speaks out for the rights of the handicapped. He draws and paints in his spare time.